ADVENTUROUS PUB WALKS

IN

WEST YORKSHIRE & THE DALES

Keith Wadd

D1335303

First published 2004
© Keith Wadd 2004

COUNTRYSIDE BOOKS
3 Catherine Road
Newbury, Berkshire

To view our complete range of books,
please visit us at
www.countrysidebooks.co.uk

ISBN 1 85306 842 X

Designed by Peter Davies, Nautilus Design
Photographs by the author

Cover photo of Oxenhope, near Keighley
supplied by Bill Meadows

Produced through MRM Associates Ltd., Reading
Typeset by Mac Style Ltd, Scarborough, N. Yorkshire
Printed by Woodnough Bookbinding Ltd., Irthlingborough

CONTENTS

Introduction 6

Walks

Holme, Hinchcliffe Mill and Hades
(9 miles) 8

Marsden, Wessenden Valley, Standedge and Tunnel End
(12 miles) 14

Stoodley Pike from Todmorden
(9 miles) 20

Hebden Bridge, Hardcastle Crags and Heptonstall
(12 miles) 26

Ledston, Aire and Calder Navigation, Fairbairn Ings and Ledsham
(10 miles) 32

Haworth, Brontë Bridge and Ponden Kirk
(9 miles) 38

Ilkley Moor from East Morton
(12 miles) 44

Bardsey, Hetchell Crags and Thorner
(10 miles) 50

Addingham to Bolton Abbey and Beamsley Beacon
(10 miles) 56

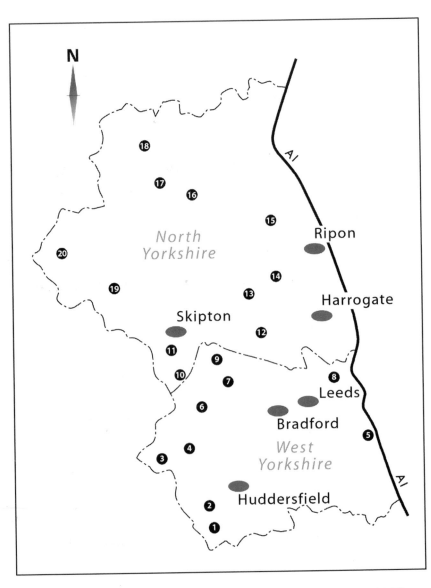

AREA MAP SHOWING THE LOCATION OF THE WALKS

Sutton-in-Craven, Slippery Ford and the Pinnacles
(12 miles) 62

Carleton, Carleton Glen and Pinhaw
(10 miles) 68

Washburn Valley Walk: Swinsty Reservoir, Lindley Wood and Dobpark Bridge
(12 miles) 74

Nidderdale Walk: Pateley Bridge, Guisecliff, Fosse Gill and Mosscar Bottom
(9 miles) 80

Fell Beck, Brimham Rocks and Eavestone Lake
(12 miles) 86

Masham, Ilton and the River Ure
(12 miles) 92

West Burton and Wensleydale Scars
(9 miles) 98

Bainbridge, Semer Water, Cragdale and Addlebrough
(14 miles) 104

Upper Swaledale from Muker
(12 miles) 110

Settle, Giggleswick Scar, Victoria Cave and Attermire Scar
(10 miles) 116

Ingleton, Clapham and Ingleborough
(12 miles) 122

INTRODUCTION

It will come as no surprise that the Yorkshire Dales is included in the title of this book of walks. It is an area of attractive and often spectacular countryside, and justly celebrated. But West Yorkshire? – isn't that Leeds, Bradford, Huddersfield, and Halifax, all joined up together in a large urban sprawl? Well, that is partly true but Yorkshire is also an area with magnificent scenery on the doorstep of every town – a landscape of steep-sided wooded valleys, reservoirs, gritstone crags, heather moors, and a mosaic of walled green fields. It is also blessed with a rich network of rights of way.

In this book, the Yorkshire Dales do not correspond exactly with the Yorkshire Dales National Park. I have included several dales – less well-known but well worth visiting – that lie just beyond its eastern boundary: Nidderdale, the Washburn Valley, Colsterdale, and the lower parts of Wensleydale and Wharfedale. I have excluded those parts of the national park that are now in Cumbria, and avoided many of the 'honeypots' like Grassington, Hawes, Kettlewell, and Malham.

Above all, I have tried to make each part of every walk in this collection an enjoyable experience. This is different from stringing together various places of special interest, which in themselves cannot compensate for an indifferent walk. If the walk has such places as well, then so much the better and their details are noted.

For me, a good walk must have variety. By this I mean, ideally, a mix of moorland or heath, field, woodland, and waterside walking; and some interesting products of human activity, such as churches, mills, monuments, and viaducts, as well as plenty of wildlife. Unfortunately, it is almost impossible to devise a good circular route without including some stretches of road. I have kept road walking to an absolute minimum, however, and what there is of it is nearly all on quiet lanes.

A good walk must also have good views. A good view need not be one that stretches for miles, but it should cause you to pause awhile to appreciate it. For a really big view, the best in this collection is from the top of Ingleborough (Walk 20), and other extensive views are to be had from Millstone Edge (Walk 2), Lund's Tower (Walk 10), Pin Haw (Walk 11), and Brimham Rocks (Walk 14). The best conditions for big views are when the wind is from the north-west or north, bringing really clean polar air. Probably the most favourable times for such conditions are in April, May, and October, but be mindful that winds from this direction usually bring showers, and these tend to be heavy and wintry, which means snow on the hills.

These walks are also designed to be 'adventurous'. I have tried to achieve this in several ways. Firstly, they are around ten miles in length; this means that they should prove a physical challenge for most people. Secondly, I have included some exciting places in most of the walks, airy spots with precipitous drops not too far from the feet. Thirdly, several of the walks are in little known locations, affording the pleasure of a new discovery.

The walks are all in lonely countryside, and, although a good pub is close by at their end, most lack such facilities en route. So; take refreshments, in particular, plenty to drink. Also important is clothing. Make sure that you take enough in case the weather turns cold, and remember that there is high and exposed ground on nearly all of the walks. A hat is recommended to keep you warm in cold weather and to protect you from the sun in hot weather. Also ensure that you have good waterproofs: jacket, overtrousers, and gloves in case of sudden downpours. A good pair of comfortable waterproof boots is a necessity. When choosing them, remember that you will be wearing two pairs of socks, including at least one thick pair. Finally, as well as the appropriate Ordnance Survey map, it is also sensible to find room in the rucksack for a compass and a whistle.

Walkers are welcome at all of the selected pubs (minus muddy boots, of course), and they can get a hot meal at all of them. At some pubs the food is fairly basic – but wholesome – though most offer both inexpensive snacks and more elaborate fare. All sell real ale and, at the time of my visit, it was in good condition. Please seek the management's permission if you would like to leave your car in the pub car park whilst you walk.

Finally, welcome to West Yorkshire and the Yorkshire Dales, and happy adventurous walking!

Keith Wadd

Dedication – This book is for all the people I have walked with over the years, both family and friends. All of them unwittingly have contributed to this collection of walks. In particular, I have much valued the help and support of Anne, my wife. I also dedicate the book to the Ramblers' Association; without their work, rights of way would be in a much worse condition and many would have been lost forever. There is still much work to be done, and all walkers are urged to join the assoication.

HOLME, HINCHCLIFFE MILL AND HADES

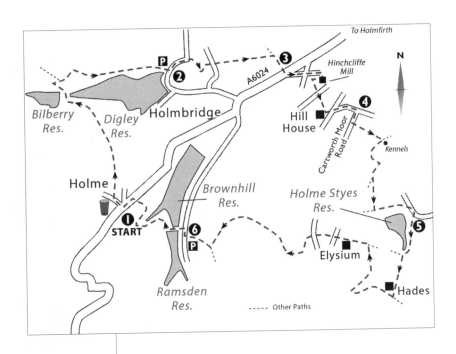

Distance:
9 miles

Starting Point:
The Fleece Inn,
Holme.
GR 107058

Map: OS Outdoor Leisure 1, Dark Peak

How to get there: The village of Holme is on the A6024, 3 miles south-west of Holmfirth and 9 miles south-west of Huddersfield. From the M1, turn off at junction 39 and follow the signs for Denby Dale and then Holmfirth. Alternatively, there is a frequent bus service from Huddersfield. The Fleece will be found on the main road in Holme. The pub car park is quite small so please obtain prior permission before leaving your car whilst you walk. There are also convenient car parks on the walk at Digley Reservoir (point 1) and Ramsden Reservoir (point 6).

HOLME STYES RESERVOIR

*T*his varied walk visits the attractive countryside at the far end of the Holme Valley, near Holmfirth. Some of the walk is in the Peak District National Park, which may come as something of a surprise in view of the fact that all of the walk is in West Yorkshire. The walk doesn't go on the high moors, but winds around the upland meadows and steep-sided tributary valleys. It goes through some fine woodland, and past several reservoirs, providing ample illustration of how they greatly enhance the scene. Above all, this is a walk on airy hillsides, with fine views down into the valleys and across to the hills and moors beyond. For much of the time the view is dominated by Black Hill (1,843 ft), whose dark presence contrasts so well with the greenery of the valley below.

Although the route does not actually take in Holmfirth, 'home' of the popular TV series *Last of the Summer Wine*, it conveys the general ambience of the countryside which forms the backcloth to the programme.

The Fleece Inn , once a livery stable for packhorses, is a popular small pub on the main road in the middle of Holme, and walkers are welcome. Meals are available from noon to 2 pm and from 6 pm to 9 pm from Tuesday to Saturday; from 6 pm to 9.30 pm on Fridays and Saturdays; and from noon to 9 pm on Sundays. The menu includes home-made steak and ale pie, which comes highly recommended, among a selection of reasonably priced main courses. On Sundays a set-price three course lunch is available, and there are tapas in the evening. The real ales are Burtonwood and two guest beers. The Fleece is closed on Mondays. Telephone: 01484 683449.

Holme, virtually the last settlement on the road to Holme Moss, is an attractive small village built in local stone; some of its houses formerly belonged to handloom weavers. This industry had its heyday in the early 1800s. The weavers' houses tended to have larger windows than the norm in order to maximise the light.

① Turn left after leaving **the Fleece**, then almost immediately left again, up the cobbled street to **Meal Hill Road**. Shortly after, by a yellow arrow and blue K on a post, turn right and go along a walled lane. Veer slightly right across a field, and continue on the clear path across several fields to the top end of **Digley Reservoir**. (There are views from the path to the Emley Moor mast and further round to the right the gorge of Ramsden Clough.)

Turn left at the junction with a well-used path, and continue along the side of the reservoir and across the dam of **Bilberry Reservoir**. Turn sharp right after the gate, and keep straight on when a lane comes in from the left. The clear path comes to a metalled road at **Digley Reservoir** car park.

② Turn left up the steep road and go over a stile by a footpath sign on the right. The path slants across the field and over a stile, and then keeps close to the wall on the right. Turn sharp left in the next field, and then go over step stiles immediately to the right of some imposing stone houses. Go across the metalled road, and continue along a walled path with fine views of **Black Hill** on the right. Keep going in the same direction across several walled fields. The wall is on the right at first, then on the left, and finally on the right again. Some stiles are marked by yellow blobs. Go slightly to the left of a house and turn right on an attractive enclosed path beside a steep-sided valley (note the mill dams). Carry straight on down the hillside on a waymarked path that becomes **Stubbin Lane** and leads to **Hinchcliffe Mill**. Note the roofed trough on the left just before the bottom.

③ Turn left for a few yards along the A6024; go down an alleyway on the right under the houses; and then turn left along the road at the back. At the crossroads, go straight on along **Water Street**, past a mill on the right, and then across a metal footbridge over the **River Holme**. Turn right almost immediately by the

side of the mill and walk round the back of it for a few yards. Then turn left up a steep shallow valley. Go through a gap stile just to the left of the stream, and continue up the hillside on a path with ancient steps. Go straight across the metalled road by a house and continue up a tree-lined path to **Hill House**. Go just to the left of the houses; then straight across up a metalled road called **Stony Gate**.

There is a good view down the valley and Jubilee Tower, only a mile and a half from the centre of Huddersfield, is particularly

THE FLEECE INN, AT THE START OF THE WALK

BLACK HILL, SEEN FROM ABOVE HINCHCLIFFE MILL

prominent. It was built in 1897 to commemorate the jubilee of Queen Victoria. Castle Hill, on which the tower is built, was an important Iron Age fort, and also the site of a Norman castle.

④ Turn right along **Cartworth Moor Road**; then turn left at a footpath sign immediately after a football pitch. The path keeps close to the wall on the left, crosses a green lane to a splendid stile of stone pillars, and then keeps close to the wall again. Go into a wood and descend steeply; then go straight across a lane and down to a row of houses.

Turn right and go past the kennels; then continue up a tree-lined lane. Where the lane leaves the trees, turn left through a gate stile, and go along a level grassy path. Go past a house on the right, then between two more houses, and continue in the same direction through a field to a wood. Turn left along an attractive path that zigzags down the valley; then go to the left of the waterworks buildings and up the steep hill at the other side. Turn right along the metalled road at the top.

⑤ Where the metalled road turns left, carry straight on along the unsurfaced lane and round the end of **Holme Styes Reservoir**. Immediately after a gate, turn left on a broad path up the hillside through extensive conifer woodlands. Turn right at the T-junction at the top, and pass the buildings at **Hades**. The path then bends round steep-sided **Reynard Clough** (where you may wish to linger at bilberry time), and goes by a wall on the left. Turn left at the junction of paths, and continue up a broad, walled lane past the farmhouse at **Elysium**. Go straight on at the junction of lanes, and when a metalled road is reached go straight across and through a metal gate. The path soon becomes a delight as it goes along the top of steep hillsides, and there are good views into the **Holme Valley**. Continue along the grassy path as it

gradually swings left, with **Black Hill** becoming increasingly prominent. Cross a stile just in front of a conifer wood; then keep the wood on your left as you descend to a metalled road beside a picnic place.

⑥ Turn right along the road, and after a short distance turn left on the footpath across the dam of **Ramsden Reservoir**. The path then veers right and follows the top of the deep wooded valley of **Rake Dike** before descending to a footbridge by an attractive waterfall. Continue along the path as it climbs the other side of the valley. It goes into an enclosed section and then a lane. (Note the interesting turf-covered house on the left.) Turn left when the A6024 is reached, and in a few yards you are back at **Holme**.

 Date walk completed:

MARSDEN, WESSENDEN VALLEY, STANDEDGE AND TUNNEL END

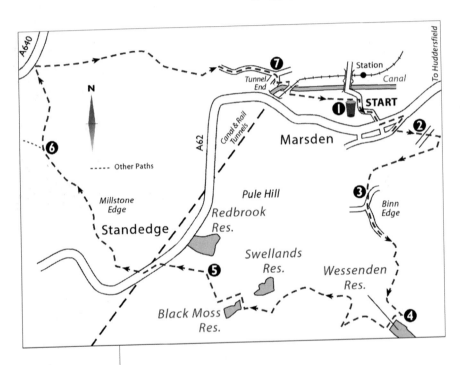

Distance:
12 miles

Starting Point:
The Railway inn at Marsden.
GR 047118

Map: OS Outdoor Leisure 21 South Pennines

How to get there: Take the A62 south-west from Huddersfield, and turn right after 7 miles into the centre of Marsden. Continue through the town and up the hill to the Railway pub, which is on the left just before the station. Alternatively, there is a frequent rail service from Leeds, Huddersfield, and Manchester.

TUNNEL END

*T*his is a fine moorland walk, full of historical interest, on a route which includes part of the Pennine Way, old turnpike roads, and an ancient packhorse track, as it winds along the side of valleys, picks its way round bumpy moorland ground, and traverses gritstone edges. It goes over the top of canal and railway tunnels, and visits Tunnel End, where they come out. There are many spectacular views, eastwards into Yorkshire and westwards into Lancashire.

The Railway pub is across the road from Marsden station and next to the canal. It is a friendly, popular, and unpretentious pub, its walls lined with interesting local pictures. It serves food daily from 9 am to 9 pm, and offers a wide range of main courses at reasonable prices. On Sundays there is a set-price three course lunch, and there is a set-price 'early bird' menu available between 4 pm and 7 pm from Monday to Friday. The real ales are Bateman's, Braines, and Burtonwood. Telephone: 01484 841541.

 The Walk

Marsden, a former mill and foundry town at the end of the Colne Valley, is a pleasant place to wander around. It is seven miles from Huddersfield and not much further from Oldham, at a point where the Pennines are at their narrowest. It is not surprising therefore that Marsden was on an obvious and popular route into Lancashire, whether over the top of the hills by packhorse track or road, or below them by canal or rail tunnel.

① On leaving the **Railway**, turn right and go down the hill. Go over the bridge and along **Peel Street** past the Marsden Mechanics' Institute and Library, an imposing stone building with a plaque inscribed *AD 1860*. Cross the A62, and continue up **Peel Street**. Turn left round the side of the park, and then after about 100 yards go up a narrow lane on the right, by G. Dyson's motor body repair shop.

The lane becomes an attractive walled lane as it climbs the hillside. When the lane turns left, go straight on through a gap stile beside a gate, and continue up the hillside on a fenced path. The path goes past a stable and onto a lane.

② Cross the lane to a National Trust sign and go over the stile beside the gate. The path winds up the side of the moor to a T-junction of paths beside a stream. Go right here on an attractive path that winds along the steep hillside, with stunning views over **Marsden** and the upper end of the **Colne Valley**. The path soon leaves the National Trust land, while continuing in the same direction along the side of the valley. It turns left at a 'no public access' sign and climbs up the hillside to a tarmac road. (There is a good view from here of **Butterley Reservoir**, the lowest of the four reservoirs in the **Wessenden Valley**.)

③ Turn right for a short distance and then left along a narrow lane at **Binn Edge**, with houses on the right and moorland on the left. The lane ends at a turning place not far beyond the houses, and there is a fine view up the **Wessenden Valley**. Take the right hand of the two paths, cross a substantial stone bridge, and then continue by a wall on the right. Go over a wooden stile by the remains of a stone house, and then over another stile shortly afterwards. Keep by the fence on the left; then slant down the hillside on a good path which soon leads to the ruins of another house. Go over a stile by a metal gate, over a broad bridge, and then a narrow vertiginous bridge. After a post with a waymark, go to the other side of a tumbledown wall, and veer slightly right to a wooden stile. In the next field, the path, now indistinct, keeps above the marshy ground on the right. After the next stile, cross the shallow valley to a waymarked post; then go to the left of a belt of trees that shelters **Wessenden Lodge**, and join the **Pennine Way** at **Wessenden Reservoir**.

④ Turn briefly right and then follow the **Pennine Way** along the dam of the reservoir, and across a concrete bridge. The attractive moorland path turns right and gently ascends a tributary valley. It fords the stream just below a waterfall, and then winds round the other side of the valley before turning into **Blakely Clough**. The stream in the clough is also forded, and then the path keeps the stream on the left as it gradually climbs up the moorland.

Pule Hill (1318 ft) dominates the scene to the right; behind you is West Nab (1509 ft); and a bit further to the right of it is Holme Moss TV mast.

The path, paved for much of the way, goes along the dam of **Black Moss Reservoir** and then swings left. **Swellands Reservoir** is nearby on the right, and you can see over to **Manchester** from here. Turn right at the junction of paths at the end of **Black Moss Reservoir**. Now continue along the **Pennine Way** towards **Redbrook Reservoir**, straight ahead.

Redbrook and Swellands reservoirs were built to provide water for the Huddersfield Narrow Canal (hundreds of feet underground at this point!).

⑤ When the path crosses a shallow stream and climbs up a bank to a stone post, turn left. You are on the 'second turnpike', that crossed the moors from Marsden to Lancashire. It is now a broad track, substantially grassed over. Soon it catches up with the 'third turnpike', now the modern A62, in a deep cutting on the right. Cross the A62 at the end of the cutting, noting the **Pennine Way** display board, and continue along a broad track. A small section of this is the 'first turnpike'. Turn right along the **Pennine Way**, whose attractive, carefully crafted route follows a low edge as it gradually ascends **Higher Standedge** and **Millstone Edge**.

There are good views on the left towards Rochdale, and the nearby green fields make a pleasant contrast with the dark moorland. From the trig point, you can see, in the opposite direction, down the Colne Valley.

⑥ When you reach a cairn and a stone post, make sure you go along the **Pennine Way** on the right. After half a mile or more, the pleasant moorland path reaches the A640. Unless you have been unable to resist the temptation to continue on the **Pennine Way** to southern Scotland, turn sharp right without crossing the A640. The path is paved for the first few yards. It climbs gently to a stone post marked 'PH road', denoting a packhorse route, and then gently descends the moor in the direction of **Marsden**, passing several more posts marked 'PH road'. This is a path to savour as it twists and turns to achieve the best dry route across the boggy terrain, whilst always staying fairly direct. Ahead there are fine views down the valley, and both **Emley Moor** TV mast and the more modestly-sized **Jubilee Tower** near Huddersfield are in view.

At the end of the moor, it is well worth spending a few minutes looking at the display board near the packhorse bridge (Close Gate Bridge). Here you will read that Marsden Town Council put up the stone posts in 1908 after a dispute with the landowner, an early example of a battle about a right of way – and one with a successful outcome.

Now go across the bridge and along the wooded path by the stream. When the metalled road is reached, turn right and continue down the valley. (Note the unusual architecture of the row of cottages on the right at **Lower Hey Green**.) Soon after, there is an old reservoir on the right, which formerly supplied the canal. As a pleasant alternative to the road, you can walk along the bank by turning right through a gap in the wall, just after the cottages.

⑦ Opposite the **Tunnel End Inn**, you take the left-hand one of the two roads that go off on the right. **Tunnel End** is just round the corner, at the bottom of the short hill. This is where the canal emerges from its long, dark journey under the moors, and just above is the entrance to the adjacent rail tunnel.

Tunnel End is a place to linger. It has great charm and also a very informative visitor centre. The canal tunnel is the older of the tunnels and took 15 years to build before its opening in 1811. Over three miles long, it is still the longest canal tunnel in England. It eventually fell into disuse and was closed in 1944, but, happily, it has now been restored and re-opened.

There are three railway tunnels, two single-track ones opened in 1849 and 1871 respectively, and the double-track tunnel opened in 1894, and used by the frequent trans-Pennine trains today. The rail tunnel entrances are quite close to the mouth of the canal tunnel.

When you need to press on with the walk, go over the canal bridge, and follow the popular towpath for half a mile to **Marsden**. You could also go by waterbus, but perhaps that would be cheating. The **Railway inn** is on the right, opposite **Marsden railway station**.

Date walk completed:

STOODLEY PIKE FROM TODMORDEN

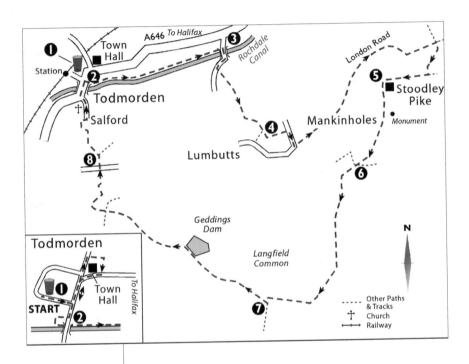

Distance:
9 miles

Starting Point:
The Queen Hotel,
Todmorden.
GR 936243

Map: OS Outdoor Leisure 21, South Pennines

How to get there: *Take the A646 along the Calder Valley from Halifax. Turn right at the main road junction in Todmorden (there is a mini roundabout), and then almost immediately turn left up to the Queen Hotel and the station. Alternatively, there is a good rail service from Leeds, Bradford, Halifax, Rochdale, and Manchester.*

STOODLEY PIKE MONUMENT

*A*fter leaving Todmorden, much of the early part of the walk is along the canal, with its varied and interesting scene. The route then turns towards Stoodley Pike, and the ascent via Lumbutts and Mankinholes – what names! – is a very gradual one, with few steep bits. The latter part of the walk, from Stoodley Pike to the other end of the moorland ridge, is enjoyable walking with many fine views, and the descent into Todmorden at the end is quite dramatic.

The Queen Hotel and Leisure Club, a residential hotel, is opposite the station. The extensive menu of main courses includes fajitas, stir fries, fillet of swordfish, and Barnsley chop. On my visit there were six real ales: Adnams, Bombardier, Landlord, J.W.Lees', Worthington, and Young's. Telephone: 01706 811500.

The Walk

Todmorden, or 'Tod', as it is familiarly called, is at the northern end of Calderdale and is a town of character and considerable interest. Until the local government reorganization of the 1970s, the county boundary went across the cricket ground, so that half of the town was in Lancashire. In the 19th century the Fielden family, local mill owners, had a major impact on the town and its architecture, and was responsible for the building of the town hall, which is particularly fine, and the Unitarian church. Sneaking right through the centre of the town, though you could easily fail to notice it if you didn't know it was there, is the Rochdale Canal, the main clue to its presence being a large bulge in Rochdale Road.

① From the **Queen Hotel**, turn left and go down **Rise Lane**. On the right is **Todmorden Hall**, an attractive building dating back to Tudor times and now housing a restaurant. Turn left and pass the parish church of St Mary, an entirely unpretentious edifice, and continue straight on for a few yards, noting the fine railway viaduct (not that you could miss it), to the main attraction: the town hall. Gazes should be directed upwards to the marble carvings. From here return to the main road junction and retrace your steps past **St Mary's church**, to the bulge in the road that conceals the **Rochdale Canal**.

The Rochdale Canal was the first of the Trans-Pennine canals and the whole route from Sowerby Bridge to Manchester was completed in 1804 (the stretch from Sowerby to Todmorden was opened six years earlier).

② Immediately before the canal bridge, turn right; this brings you to **Todmorden Lock** (no.19), a pleasant bit of urban canal scenery. Turn sharp left under the bridge, and continue along the canalside path for about a mile. The water is unpolluted, and as well as boat life, there are ducks and geese, and often, people fishing. Interspersed with various factories and industrial units, there is plenty of pleasant canal architecture to enjoy – **Old Royd Lock** (no.17) is a particularly attractive place.

③ When you come to a tall black chimney to the right of the canal, turn left up the steps, immediately after going under a bridge, and then turn left along the road and over the canal. The large building on the left is former **Woodhouse Mill**, now converted into an apartment block – a sign of the times. Continue up the road past the chimney, and turn left up a track between houses, signed '**Calderdale link path**' (just before **Cherry Tree Cottage**). Where the

path divides – there are footpath signs for both – take the enclosed path which carries straight on. This soon emerges into open fields as it climbs the hillside. There are good views behind to the upper part of the **Calder Valley. Stoodley Pike** comes into view again and more or less straight ahead is **Lumbutts Mill**, which looks like a gigantic version of an early mobile phone. The clear path, flagged in places, turns right and goes between cottages before coming out at the **Top Brink Inn**.

You may wish to go down the walled path on the right to have a

THE QUEEN HOTEL SEEN FROM TODMORDEN HALL

closer look at the mill (now The Lumbutts Centre), which housed three water wheels. There is an informative noticeboard, but the mill is private.

④ Immediately after the **Top Brink Inn**, turn left along a flagged path which leads into **Mankinholes** at the top of the field. Turn right through the stone village of former weavers' houses, and note the magnificent horse troughs. Immediately after the troughs, turn left along a walled lane, now part of the **Pennine Bridleway**. This is **London Road**. Soon there is open moorland on the right, and all along there are magnificent views of **Stoodley Pike Monument**. The track is level for a while and then climbs gently as it swings round to the back of the monument. Turn right and go onto the **Pennine Way** at the signpost just before the farm at **Swillington**, and climb up the hillside to a step stile.

Stoodley Pike Monument rears up close by, and in a few minutes you are there. (The impatient ones may turn off London Road at an earlier point and make a more direct ascent.)

Stoodley Pike Monument was erected in 1815 to mark the end of the Napoleonic Wars. The view is excellent, though not particularly extensive. Thieveley Pike, not far from Burnley, is prominent to the west, and further round to the north is Boulsworth Hill. A shade east of north is the tower of Heptonstall church, and further round to the east is the wind farm on Ovenden Moor, near Halifax. In the foreground is an attractive pattern of green meadows and parallel dark walls. The chilly platform part way up the monument doesn't add to the view, but the dark stone staircase to get there is a minor adventure in itself.

Without the monument, Stoodley Pike would just be an ordinary Pennine hillside, and we would scarcely give it a second glance. Monuments such as this embellish many a peak and hillside in the southern Pennines.

⑤ From the monument, continue on the **Pennine Way** along the moorland edge, with good views down into the valley.

⑥ After two thirds of a mile the **Pennine Way** is crossed by a marvellous example of a flagged packhorse track. (It is worth walking down it to the first corner just to appreciate it.) Continue along the **Pennine Way**, which descends to a shallow valley and then climbs the hillside, passing a stone seat with the charming dedication 'Cyril Webster, still walking the hills'. The well-used path continues southwards across the moor and then swings right alongside **Warland Drain**.

⑦ Immediately after the **Pennine Way** turns sharp left over a stone bridge, turn right on a paved path across boggy moorland towards a large sheet of water, which is **Geddings Dam**. It comes as quite a surprise to see a large reservoir on the top of a moor. Go along the side of the dam as far as the corner, and then bear left down an attractive moorland path. (The **Basin Stone** is passed on the left and there are fine views of **Gorpley Valley** straight ahead.) After crossing the **Pennine** bridleway, the path swings round to the right and goes through a metal gate into a walled lane. Take care on the mossy flagstones as you descend the lane. Immediately before the house, turn right by a footpath sign, and go down the side of the garden

and into a field. Cross a road and keep beside a wall on the right; then go through a gap stile into a lane.

⑧ Turn left, and follow **Shoebroad Lane** through the other **Salford** and down the hill towards **Todmorden**. The impressive spire of the Unitarian church is straight ahead. The descent becomes steep and dramatic, with **Todmorden** town hall and the viaduct also coming into view.

The Unitarian church, now a listed building, is passed on the left. It was built in 1869, and can be viewed by arrangement (details on the gate).

Turn right when you come to **Fielden Square** at the bottom of the hill and walk along **Rochdale Road** into the centre of the town.

Date walk completed:

HEBDEN BRIDGE, HARDCASTLE CRAGS AND HEPTONSTALL

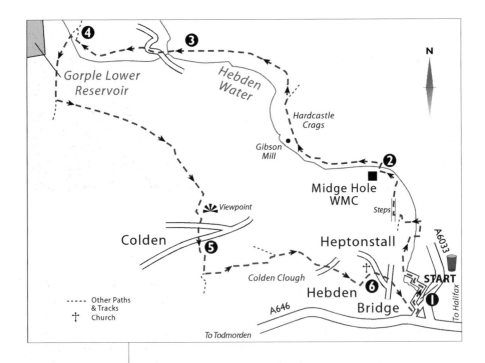

Distance:
12 miles

Starting Point:
The White Lion at
Hebden Bridge.
GR 993273

Map: OS Outdoor Leisure 21, South Pennines

How to get there: *Take the A646 westwards along the
Calder Valley from Halifax, and at the traffic lights in the
middle of Hebden Bridge, turn right along Bridge Gate.
The White Lion is on the left at the top of Bridge Gate.
There is a good rail service to Hebden Bridge from Leeds,
Bradford, Halifax, and Lancashire.*

THE WOODED VALLEY OF HEBDEN WATER

*T*his is as good a walk as you will find anywhere. It starts at Hebden Bridge and goes up the steep-sided valley of Hebden Water, the fast-flowing stream that can be heard at the side of the White Lion. Much of the valley is covered by the woodlands of the National Trust's Hardcastle Crags estate, and these provide some delightful walking. The route climbs out of the woodland and onto the moors, where there are many breathtaking views. Later on, we follow the rocky, well-wooded edge of Colden Clough, and the final part of this walk takes us to Heptonstall. This is one of the most interesting villages in the Pennines; so allow time to browse. Passing over packhorse bridges and along flagged tracks, we are reminded of a way of life in which the wheel was of only limited use and nearly all movement on the steep hillsides was by horse or on foot.

The White Lion Hotel is a Grade 2 listed building and dates back to 1658. The main courses at this residential hotel are reasonably priced and the daily menu includes many specials. Food is available between noon and 8 pm, Monday to Saturday; and from noon to 2.30 pm and from 7 pm to 9 pm on Sundays. The real ales at the time of writing were Boddington's, Castle Eden, Deuchars', Flowers', Landlord, and Whittaker's. Telephone: 01422 842197.

The first thing that I always notice in Hebden Bridge are the rows of four-storey terraces lining the steep valley. The four storeys actually contain two houses, the first reached at the ground floor on the lower side of the building, and the second reached at third storey level on the other side of the building. Hebden Bridge was formerly an industrial town, and in the valley were many mills. Some of the chimneys still remain. Today, with industry in the conventional sense long since departed, Hebden Bridge is a popular place to live for people who appreciate the uniqueness of its appearance and its attractive wooded surroundings. It is also popular with visitors.

① Go along **Valley Road** to the right of **Hebden Bridge** marketplace, past the fire station and the children's playground. Take the second street on the right

(**Windsor Road**), and the first left (**Windsor Place**), which soon leads to an attractive packhorse bridge over the river. The scenery has now changed from town to country. Turn right immediately after the bridge on an attractive path signed **'Riverside Path Hardcastle Crags'**. Ignore the Riverside Path route over the footbridge, and go on the track straight ahead. Where the tracks divide, continue along the one marked 'private road public footpath'. Immediately after it takes a sharp hairpin bend to the left, go up the narrow walled path on the right which climbs the steep hillside by a series of stone steps. Turn right at the top along a narrow metalled road. There are many handsome hollies in the adjacent wood. Turn down the track by the wall and descend to the valley bottom. Go past **Midge Hole Working Men's Club**, and then cross the river by the fine arched bridge.

② Turn left immediately after the bridge by the National Trust notice for **Hardcastle Crags**. For the next mile, just follow the path up the valley to **Gibson Mill**.

This is a delightful wooded path, never far away from the sound of the stream. Beeches and oaks are the main deciduous trees, but contrast is provided by the many Scots pines. It is a justly popular area. Many people bring their dogs, so that on a fine Sunday morning the valley is a sort of sylvan Cruft's.

Gibson Mill, built in 1800 as a water-powered cotton mill, was later used as a roller-skating rink and dance hall, according to the display board.

Take the crushed stone track to the right of the mill, which climbs gradually up the valley side. (Behind the wooded hillocks on the left are **Hardcastle Crags**.) Take the broad track to the left by a post with a green mark (a few yards further on there is a gate with a letterbox). After about a mile, the track leaves the woodland, passes a cottage, and continues along the hillside. It briefly goes through more woodland, and then twists around the humps and hollows of old quarry workings.

HEBDEN BRIDGE

Down in the valley are the abutments of a former railway viaduct, part of a network of railway lines used in the construction of the reservoirs further up the valley. The scene is delightful, and I marvel at how quickly nature can transform a landscape.

③ Follow the path as it descends to a footbridge and comes out on the road to **Colne**. Turn right and then go through the stile on the left at the hairpin bend. The path gradually climbs the low gritstone edge, and then goes along an old wall at the top, before coming to the **Pennine Way**. The white building on the right is the **Pack Horse Inn**, where there are photographs of the former railways.

④ Turn sharp left down the flagged **Pennine Way** as it drops into a beautiful valley and climbs steeply up the other side. Carry straight on past the signpost and continue up the hillside, with views of **Gorple Lower Reservoir** on the right. Immediately after the gate, turn left on the **Pennine Way**, along the side of the moor.

To the left is a splendid south Pennine scene of green meadows, dark walls, moorland, patches of woodland, and occasional farmsteads. The highest point, well round to the left, is Boulsworth Hill

(1,564 ft). The whole moorland was important in the long – and eventually successful – Right to Roam campaign. Further on, the tower of Heptonstall church comes into view.

On the latter part of the moor, the path (still the **Pennine Way**) veers away from the wall on the left and heads towards the farmhouse on the near horizon. The path goes just to the right of the farmhouse, and immediately after there is an excellent viewpoint. Go through a gate close to the wall on the left, descend to a narrow metalled road and then to a wider metalled road (which leads to **Burnley**).

⑤ Cross the road and keep straight on down the **Pennine Way**. The path goes through a plethora of gates as it goes round the left-hand side of the house at the bottom of the lane, and then crosses a small field to the bottom left-hand corner. It then descends a walled path before entering the woodland of **Colden Clough**. Leave the **Pennine Way** after a few yards, and turn left along an attractive flagged path. This goes through a beech wood (ignore the path on the right down into the valley) and then, still flagged, crosses several fields in the direction of **Heptonstall**. Turn right by the footpath sign at the T-junction of lanes, and then go to the immediate left of a house and along another flagged path. There is a fine view down **Colden Clough**. At the junction of paths, go slightly right (to the right of the Scots pine), and keep by the wall on the left when the path divides. Go up the metalled road straight ahead, then right at the 'public footpath Heptonstall' sign, and into **Eaves Wood**. Turn left at the post where the path divides and then enjoy a marvellous stretch of walking. The path keeps close to the top of the wood as it winds amongst large rocks. There is then an exhilarating and mildly vertiginous stretch as it runs along a rocky edge, with exciting views across the valley and over to **Stoodley Pike Monument**. Now turn left along a walled lane between modern houses and follow it into **Heptonstall**.

⑥ Just before the church, turn left up a walled lane, and then turn right into the churchyard.

In the newer graveyard, over the wall on the left, the poet Sylvia Plath is buried in a very unpretentious plot that takes some finding. As you round the tower of Heptonstall church, you will be surprised to see another church, now in ruins, in front of you. This is the old church, dating from the 13th century. In 1847 it was badly damaged in a storm and was replaced by the new church, whose tower has graced the Pennine landscape ever since.

Go to the right of the old church and past the former grammar school, which houses the museum. The village was a centre of handloom weaving, and many of the weavers'cottages survive. The path goes under a stone arch and on to **Towngate**, the cobbled main street. Turn right and pass the **Cross Inn**.

Along Northgate, which goes off to the left, is the octagonal Methodist church, whose foundation stone was laid by John Wesley.

Continue down **Towngate**, past the post office, and down the road towards **Hebden Bridge**. After 300 yards or so, turn left down down a steep path with steps and a handrail. Turn right for a few yards at the bottom, and then left down a steep cobbled lane, marked (quite correctly) as unsuitable for motors, which very rapidly descends into **Hebden Bridge**. (Use of the handrail is recommended.) Cross the fine packhorse bridge and turn left to the **White Lion**.

Date walk completed:

LEDSTON, AIRE AND CALDER NAVIGATION, FAIRBURN INGS AND LEDSHAM

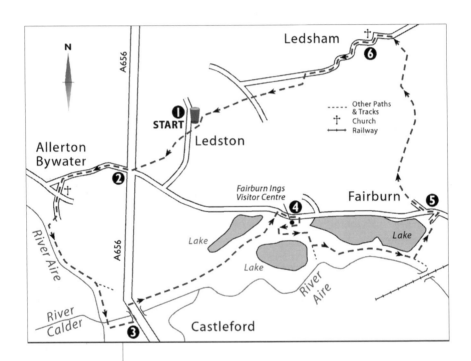

Distance:
10 miles

Map: OS Explorer 289, Leeds

Starting Point:
The White Horse
at Ledston.
GR 433286

How to get there: *Ledston is 2¹/₂ miles north of Castleford. Turn off the M62 for Castleford at junction 31 or 32. Go north out of Castleford on the A656; then, after just over a mile, turn right at the traffic lights and then left for Ledston. Point 3 of the walk is less than a mile from Castleford railway station.*

THE AIRE AND CALDER NAVIGATION

*T*his walk takes us through an attractive hotchpotch of a landscape, a mix of industrial and rural, and its charm lies in its variety and its many features of interest. Part of the route is beside the Aire and Calder Navigation, a canal with commercial barges nipping along at a fair rate of knots, and for three miles the walk goes through the RSPB's nature reserve at Fairburn Ings. On the latter part of the walk, there is some attractive, well-wooded traditional countryside on the narrow belt of magnesium limestone that runs through Yorkshire on its way from Nottinghamshire to the Durham coast.

En route we visit four villages and pass close to the town of Castleford, a former Roman settlement (*Lagentium*). Many of the houses in Ledston, Fairburn and Ledsham are built in local limestone and contrast with the brick buildings of the former mining village of Allerton Bywater. The imposing chimney and cooling towers of Ferrybridge Power Station – still fed by coal – are frequently visible.

The White Horse on the main street in the village of Ledston is deservedly popular. The pub is built in the local limestone and is over 200 years old. It is full of interesting photographs of Ledston and its surroundings in the recent past. On the menu is a wide range of appetizing main courses – try the seafood en croute or the lamb shank – and there are also curries, pasta, and pizza. Food is served all day on Saturday, from 11 am to 11 pm, and on Sunday from 11 am to 10.30 pm. From Monday to Friday food is available from noon to 2.15 pm and from 6 pm in the evening. The real ales are Black Sheep, Simpson and Simpson, and Speckled Hen. Telephone: 01977 553069.

The Walk

① Turn left down the village street after leaving **The White Horse**. Just before the speed derestriction signs, turn right at a public footpath sign. The path keeps close to a fence on the left, and goes through a kissing gate and over a footbridge.

From the first field there are good views back to Ledston Hall, a large, impressive mansion in white local stone, on a ridge overlooking the valley. Most of it was built in the 1500s and 1600s on the site of an early medieval chapel and has recently been converted to apartments.

② Cross the main **A656** (a former Roman road going north from Castleford), and go along the road into **Allerton Bywater**. On the left was the colliery.

Not long ago the appearance and social fabric of Allerton Bywater and much of the surrounding area were massively dominated by coal. Spoil heaps and winding gear were a major feature in the landscape. Today, if you didn't know where the pit in Allerton Bywater used to be, you would be hard pressed to find it. But this is no cause for rejoicing. Coal mining dominated the employment structure too; when the pits closed, the effect was savage, and the lives of many individuals and families have still not recovered.

Turn left along **Vicars Terrace** to the church of **St Mary the Less** (with a lychgate proclaiming 'Death, the Gate of Life'), cross the road and go along **Main Street**. Immediately after a tall thin house opposite the Victoria Hotel, turn right across open ground to the **River Aire** and turn left along the attractive riverbank. The path passes The Boat inn (also to be recommended), and continues as a paved walk along the high riverbank. Keep to the riverbank when the paved path swings left, and soon the path comes to a waterway junction with a signpost for canal traffic. Go over a large metal bridge which crosses the canal, signed to Goole. This is a pleasant place to pause and enjoy the unusual scene, and convenient seats are provided nearby. One is dedicated to Eric Barker of the Ramblers' Association, who did a lot of work in helping to keep local footpaths open. Continue along the right-hand bank of the canal and pause again for a few minutes, this time to read the

display board on the history of the Aire and Calder Navigation.

③ When the path joins the **A656**, go left over the bridge, and then turn right on an access road by the canal. (Note the wharves at the far side of the canal; Castleford is still an inland port.) Continue along the road and past a large chemical works on the other side of the water. When **Bulholme Lock** is reached, turn left by the sign for a public footpath to Newton. The path soon turns left over an ugly concrete bridge, and then sharp right and under the bridge of the former

LEDSTON

railway to Allerton Bywater. Continue in the same direction and along a faint path immediately to the right of a hawthorn hedge. The air is full of the cries of birds on the nearby lake. The path goes over a stile and then along a fence on the right. At the end of the field, there is a stile by a gate at the end of a row of hawthorns. Slant across the next field to a stile onto the road. (If you look back, there is a wide view over to the Pennines with the Emley Moor mast.) Now turn right along the road to the RSPB car park at **Fairburn Ings**.

At the visitor reception building, you can find out about the reserve and its development, its birds and other wildlife, and the particular birds to look out for. Without coal mining, the reserve would not be there; all the lakes and wetlands occurred because of mining subsidence, and much of the rest of the reserve has been landscaped from colliery spoil. Trees and bushes have grown on the banks by the lakes, and now the extensive reserve is a place of beauty.

④ Follow the signs to **Pickup hide** on a path through attractive woodland, and then continue round the circuit of the reserve, passing the bird feeding station and interesting information boards. Follow the riverside trail through a gate and

across former mine workings, and then turn left over a stile. The path soon leads to a high wooded bank with a large lake on the left and the **River Aire** on the right, a beautiful stretch of walking. After a mile, the path drops down between gorse bushes, with the three-arched railway bridge over the river straight ahead. Turn left here along a broad straight track beside the lake, which eventually becomes **Cut Road** and leads to a T-junction in the middle of **Fairburn**.

⑤ Turn left along the road at the T-junction, and then turn up **Beckfield Lane** on the right. After 200 yards, turn right by a public footpath sign, along a wooded lane. Go through a metal kissing gate and keep close to a fence on the left. The path is on a low escarpment, and there are good views across the valley. After the third kissing gate, the path goes into a meadow, with the fence now on the right. It is attractive countryside of woodland, fields, and low hills. Veer left just before going under the power lines, and cross the field to a kissing gate. Go through the short belt of woodland, and then cross the field to a gap in the far left corner. After 100 yards, go over a stile into wood on the right. The clear path keeps fairly close to the edge of the wood and then emerges in a field. It continues in the same direction along a farm track and past some fine mature beeches before coming out onto a road. (Note the boulders of local limestone.)

⑥ Turn left into **Ledsham**, with a fine view of the church spire straight ahead.

By far the most interesting building on the walk, the church at Ledsham is probably the oldest church in West Yorkshire. The bottom part of the tower is Saxon, and so is the attractive low doorway. The stone carvings round the doorway are a Victorian restoration. The interior is also of interest, particularly the tombs, one of which belongs to Lady Mary Bolles, whose ghost is said still to walk the village.

Now continue through the village past the **Chequers Inn** and along **Claypit Lane**. Keep on the road for half a mile, taking care on the blind bends, and then take the second footpath on the left into a wood. The well-marked, attractive path now makes a beeline for **Ledston**, crossing two fields, a metalled road, and then running beside a hedge on the right. Keep in the same direction through a belt of sycamores and across a meadow close to the stone-built riding stables of **Ledston Hall**. Finally, go down the enclosed path beside a wood, and turn left along a tree-lined lane leading straight to **The White Horse**.

Date walk completed:

HAWORTH, BRONTË BRIDGE AND PONDEN KIRK

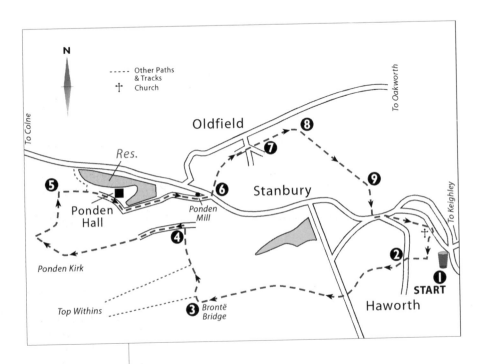

Distance:
9 miles

Starting Point:
Haworth Old Hall inn car park. GR 032369

Map: OS Outdoor Leisure 21 South Pennines

How to get there: *Haworth is 4 miles south-west of Keighley. From Keighley, take the A629 towards Halifax. At crossroads turn right along the A6033, and then continue along the B6142 to Haworth. Haworth Old Hall is on Sun Street, at the bottom of the main tourist street. You can also arrive at Haworth in style by steam train on the Keighley and Worth Valley Railway; Haworth station is 10 minutes from the start of the walk.*

VIEW TOWARDS TOP WITHINS

*T*he walk goes on the moors close to Haworth and gives a very good feel of the setting of Emily Brontë's famous novel *Wuthering Heights*. Part of the moorland route includes an adventurous path round the edge of the deep valley of Ponden Kirk. The return goes on some little used paths near Oldfield and crosses a packhorse bridge in a beautiful setting. Top Withins is not included on the route, but those who wish to visit it can extend the walk by continuing up the valley after Brontë Bridge.

The featured pub, **Haworth Old Hall**, is a former manor house dating back to 1612. It offers a wide range of reasonably priced main courses, including fish dishes and pasta dishes. Food is served from noon to 2.30 pm and from 5.30 pm to 9 pm from Monday to Saturday, and from noon to 8 pm on Sunday. The real ales are Jennings'. Telephone: 01535 642709.

The Walk

Haworth, at the start of the walk, is of course the Brontë village. Although it is a large Pennine village sprawling up both sides of the valley, tourist attention is focused on just one small part consisting of Main Street. This is a narrow cobbled street, close to the edge of the moors and is lined with shops, cafés, and pubs. At the top is the parish church and the parsonage where the Brontë family lived, and which now houses a museum. The museum is well worth a visit, as it is informative, full of interesting memorabilia, and refreshingly gimmick free.

① Walk up **Main Street**, and then turn left up the steps to **Haworth church**. At the top of the steps, turn left along a flagged path which goes through the churchyard. (All of the Brontë family except Anne are buried here.) The path continues along the hillside, with chicken runs over the fence on the left. Turn right and go up a stony lane which runs inside an avenue of sycamores.

② Cross a road, and go onto the moor. Take the left-hand of the two signed paths, directing you along the **Brontë Way** to **Brontë Falls** and **Top Withins**. The broad path, which climbs gently at first and then levels out, goes to the right of a low moorland ridge; the walking is easy and the views are excellent.

Straight ahead is the upper part of the Worth Valley, with the distinctive top of Pendle Hill just beyond; and Ponden Clough is a little to the left. Further to the left is the valley of South Dean Beck leading up to Top Withins.

When a footpath signpost is reached after about half a mile, ignore the **Brontë Way**, which turns off to the right, and briefly go straight on, along the route signed 'Oxenhope and toilets' (the latter long since boarded up). After just a few yards, slant right along a faint track that soon comes to a metalled road. Go straight across to the public footpath sign, and continue across the moor on a good clear path. This eventually joins up with the **Brontë Way** again, and continues alongside a narrowing valley before dropping to **Brontë**

Bridge, an attractive and justly popular spot.

There are tinkling streams racing over the rocks, wooded hillsides, and a splendid stone clapper bridge. Nearby, up the tributary valley to the left are the Brontë Falls.

③ Go over the bridge and zigzag up the steep hillside to a plethora of footpath signs. Turn right at the first signpost, along '**Brontë Way, Stanbury, Haworth**'; then turn right at the next one, similarly signed. Go round a corner to signpost 3; then veer right and go over a ladder stile into a field. At signpost 4 in the field, turn left along '**Brontë Way, Wycoller**', and then go over a ladder stile onto the moor again. (There are good views of the surrounding moors and the village of **Stanbury**, and down the **Worth Valley**.) Carry straight on at the next signpost and straight on at the next (signpost 6), where you come onto the **Pennine Way**. The path continues through an attractive walled section, at the end of which there are good views of **Ponden Clough** to the left, and then drops down to an unsurfaced road.

THE PUB IN HAWORTH

④ Turn left along the road; then, after a third of a mile, go over a stile at the side of a house, **Far Slack**, and onto the moor. Keep close to a wall on the right as far as a signpost; then continue in the same direction across the open moor. This is an enjoyable moorland path, well-trodden enough to be distinct, but not enough to be eroded. It climbs gradually up the side of **Stanbury Moor** and comes out on the edge of **Ponden Clough**. Care is needed here, as the path is never far from steep drops on the right. Ford the stream – some care needed here, too – and at the signpost go left and zigzag up the hillside. The path winds round the top of the clough and passes **Ponden Kirk**, a large gritstone crag, just to the right of the path. It fords another stream, and then swings right along the edge of the clough for 200 yards or so. Keep close to a wall on the right as the path descends rough pastureland; then go straight down the field to a stile over the wall – this stile also needs care. Continue in the same direction to the bottom of the hill, where the **Brontë Way** is met again.

⑤ Turn right along the **Brontë Way**, passing a house and going into a green lane. Keep going in the same direction when the path is joined by the Pennine Way, and go along a narrow tarmac road past **Ponden Hall**, a fine 17th-century farmhouse, which is reputedly the Thrushcross

Grange of *Wuthering Heights*. Keep along the road by the side of **Ponden Reservoir**, ignoring the Pennine and Brontë ways going off on the right, and go down the valley past **Ponden Mill** (circa 1793), now a very substantial commercial enterprise, with refreshments available.

⑥ Go straight across the **Haworth–Colne road**, and through a stile by a footpath sign. Walk beside the **River Worth** for a few yards, go over a stile, and then keep by a hedge on the right. Turn up the bank on the left to a stile, and continue in the same direction on a clear path up the hillside and to the right of a farm. (Glance back for good views of **Ponden Clough**.) The path goes though a farm gate at the top of the second field, and another farm gate after the third field. Cross to a footpath gate at the far side of the fourth field, and then keep beside a wall on the right. The path goes just to the left of **Oldfield End Farm**, and then across two step stiles and onto an access road. You are now in **Oldfield**.

⑦ At the junction of access roads, go straight ahead through a large stone gap stile, and cross a short field, keeping close to the wall on the right. At the end of the field, go through an unusual stone stile, and then turn right along an access road, which almost immediately bends round to the left. Ignoring the yellow arrow pointing to the right, go just to the left of the house straight ahead of you. Now keep straight ahead through a narrow gate, and continue in exactly the same direction through gardens and close to houses on the left. After the last house, continue in the same direction across small fields, and then after a farm gate steer slightly left to a gate in the middle of the farm buildings at **West House Farm**. The path goes to the side of the gate and then straight on and through a stile into the farmyard. Keeping the farm buildings on your right, carry on in the same direction for a short distance to a gate, and shortly afterwards to a stile into a field. (This section can be very muddy in winter.) Keep close to the wall in the field, and then slant slightly right to a newly constructed stile to the right of some tall hollies in the hedge.

⑧ Turn right down **Street Lane**, but take the left one of the two options and go to the left of the house. Go over a stile and down what has now become an attractive green lane. Ignore paths to the left and right, and continue in the same direction over a stile into a large field. Keep close to the left-hand fence and descend the field to a stile in the bottom left-hand corner. A few yards ahead, in a delightful sylvan setting, is a fine packhorse bridge, **Long Bridge**, beside a ford.

⑨ Cross the bridge and then walk beside the stream for a few yards. The path now climbs up the left-hand side of the field to a stile at **Lower Oldfield Farm**. Keep the house on your left, and climb steeply up a lane. Turn left along the road at the top, and after a short distance go through a stile on the right, just after a bus stop. The attractive flagged path goes across a field and soon leads into **Haworth**, close to the **Brontë Museum**. Walk down **Main Street** to **Haworth Old Hall**.

Date walk completed:

ILKLEY MOOR FROM EAST MORTON

WHITE WELLS ON ILKLEY MOOR

Distance:
12 miles

Starting Point:
The Busfeild Arms,
East Morton near
Keighley.
GR 098419

Map: OS Outdoor Leisure 21 South Pennines

How to get there: *East Morton is 2 miles north of Bingley. Go along the A650 on the new Bingley relief road. Turn right at the first roundabout and right again at the roundabout immediately after, and then turn left up a lane signed 'Morton'. Turn right at the mini-roundabout in East Morton and The Busfeild Arms is on the left, 200 yards further on.*

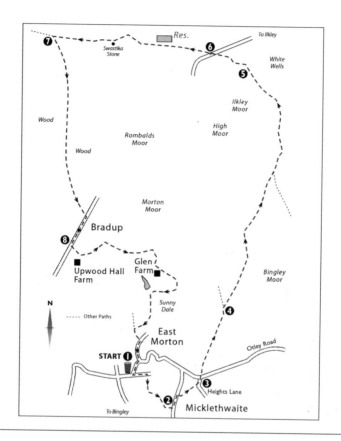

A walk on Ilkley Moor is a must, if only because it is the most famous moor in Yorkshire. The route begins at the village of East Morton, built on a hillside overlooking the Aire Valley, just a few miles from the centre of Bradford. It then goes through the nearby village of Micklethwaite before crossing Ilkley Moor on a splendid moorland path with ever-changing views. Though it can easily be extended to do so, the walk does not go into Ilkley town, but turns towards the edge of Addingham High Moor, passing the well-known Swastika Stone. The return journey takes us southwards across a narrower section of moorland, through an extensive wood, and finally down Sunny Dale, which is at the head of the valley of Morton Beck.

The Busfeild Arms at East Morton is a popular village pub. It offers a wide range of hot platters and other main courses, including 8 oz rump and gammon steaks. Meals are available from Monday to Friday, from noon to 2 pm and from 5.30 pm to 8 pm, and on Saturday and Sunday from noon to 5 pm. The real ales are Bass, Pedigree, Stones, and Tetley's. Telephone: 01274 550931.

 The Walk

① From the **Busfeild Arms**, go straight across the road and down **Dimples Lane**. Shortly after Dimples Lane becomes **Cliffe Mill Fold**, turn right down a narrow passageway. This immediately leads onto an attractive wooded path, which crosses **Morton Beck** by a footbridge and continues along a walled lane. It soon leads to a row of houses at **Beck Farm Barn** and then comes out onto the main street of **Micklethwaite**.

② Turn left up the steep main street and pass the small village green. Just before the speed de-restriction signs, there is a metal footpath gate between two gates on the right, the upper gate marked 'Tanelorn and Bank End', and the lower one 'Whins Cottage'.

(Now comes an adventurous section of the walk, and you might get your feet wet (or even your knees); so, if you are worried, carry straight on up the road, and then turn right at the top along **Otley Road** until you

reach **Heights Lane** coming in from the right.)

For those who are prepared to risk taking a more pleasant and interesting route, go through the metal gate and slant up the hillside by the first powerline post. Go to the right of the silver birches and then to a stile at the top left-hand corner of the field, close to a hawthorn bush. Keep in the same direction in the next field to a stile that leads into a marshy enclosed section, and then go over another stile on the right. The challenge is to cross the next few yards. Of the several routes I have tried, the best is to follow the arrow on the stile and go straight across the narrowest section of the bog to a rock near the corner of the wall. It helps to tread on the thick clumps of marsh grass, as they are usually firm and above the waterline. Now strike left up the field on a line to the left of the wood. Go over a stone stile and turn left along **Heights Lane** to a T-junction.

③ Go straight across the T-junction (or, for those on the alternative route, turn left) to a metal gate stile beside the right-hand farm gate. Follow the track beside the wood onto a splendid moorland route, with vista after vista unfolding as you go along.

In the foreground the meadows in the valley of Fenny Shaw Beck contrast with the dark moorland. Further afield, there is a dramatic view over Keighley and beyond that to the Brontë moors. Pendle Hill, away to the west, becomes increasingly prominent.

④ Veer right after two thirds of a mile onto a path between two low stone posts (an arrow and 'Ilkley' is painted on one of them). The path eventually comes to a wall and keeps to the right of it. Look back when you reach the stile for good views down into **Bradford** and **Leeds**. (The well-known Lister Mills chimney can be seen just to the right of Bradford city centre.) Keep straight on when a wide cross-path is met just after the stile. (There is now a wide view across **Wharfedale**, stretching from **Barden Moor** to the white radar discs on **Menwith Hill**.) The path joins the popular route from **Dick Hudsons pub** and continues in the same direction. You are now unequivocally on **Ilkley Moor**.

THE BUSFEILD ARMS

Ilkley Moor is a small part of a large expanse of wild and lonely moorland that also includes Addingham High Moor, Bingley Moor, Burley Moor, Hawksworth Moor, Morton Moor, Rombalds Moor (this is the most extensive one), and two High Moors. The whole is popularly referred to as Ilkley Moor, though this doesn't suit purists. The moorland is of considerable antiquarian interest, and the Swastika Stone (point 6) and the many cup and ring rock carvings are thought to date back to the 4th century BC.

Fairly soon, the path begins to drop steeply to the attractive white-painted house at **White Wells**.

This is where the waters which led to Ilkley's development as a spa were first discovered. The building contains one of the baths, and around it is a small exhibition describing the history of White Wells. There is also a café.

(Those with the time and energy may now choose to go down one of the several paths into **Ilkley**, a pleasant, spaciously laid out town with Roman origins. The route can be rejoined at 6.)

⑤ By the toilets at **White Wells**, join a broad path along the hillside. Just after a small valley which the path crosses by a substantial bridge,

turn left by a post, and continue along the hillside. When the path divides, go left along an attractive sunken track through bracken.

⑥ Go straight across the metalled road to a footpath sign, cross a stone footbridge, and continue in the same direction on a clear path with a wall on the right. The path passes a reservoir on the right and then crosses a footbridge at an attractive spot. Shortly after this, ignore the path into the wood to **Hebers Ghyll**, and keep along the wall to a metal gate. Turn briefly left here, under an oak tree, and then go along a path climbing gently towards some railings which guard the **Swastika Stone**. Continue westward on an enjoyable path along the gritstone edge, with fine views of **Wharfedale** and **Beamsley Beacon**. After the belt of larch trees, note the stiles carefully: first there is a disused one by a gap in the wall, then you go over a stone step stile, and then shortly afterwards through a metal gate.

⑦ Just before a second metal gate, turn sharp left on a path, indistinct at first, leading to a stile in the wall about 200 yards further on. Cross the stile and go straight ahead – don't slant left – and make for a shallow cleavage in the hillside. The path then becomes clear, swings slightly left, and makes for the gap in the wood ahead. Cross the wall by a ladder stile, and continue in the same direction through the thick evergreen wood. The path is a dark and often muddy tunnel – quite an unusual, even eerie, walking experience. When you eventually come out onto the moor again, carry straight on. The heather is growing over the path, but you can still feel the path with your feet as the heather brushes your shins, and there is a white post to guide you. The twisting path eventually leads to a stile. The path in the next field soon peters out, but make for a gate to the left of the house at **Bradup**, and then turn right along the metalled road.

⑧ Turn left at a public bridleway sign, and go past **Upwood Hall Farm** on the right and through two farm gates. Immediately before the next gate, turn left, following the waymark arrow, and go along a track beside the wall. This is a pleasant walk along upland meadows; it is fairly easy to follow and there are good views. When two gates confront you just after a shallow valley, go through the right-hand one and keep close to the wall on the left. The path swings round to the right after the second shallow valley and goes down by the side of a stone barn. Slant left across the field to a gap in the wall and then follow the track to a gate to the left of **Glen Farm**. Turn left along the access road, which descends into wooded **Sunny Dale** and across the bottom of a dam. It continues through fields, with good views down the valley of **Morton Beck**. At the junction of tracks near **Moorfield Farm**, turn left down the lane, which fairly soon leads to the main street in **East Morton**. Turn right and shortly you will be back at the **Busfeild Arms**.

Date walk completed:

BARDSEY, HETCHELL CRAGS AND THORNER

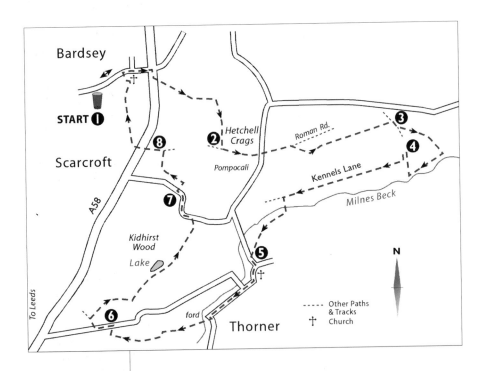

Distance:
10 miles

Starting Point:
The Bingley Arms
at Bardsey.
GR 365432

Map: OS Explorer 289, Leeds

How to get there: Bardsey is 8 miles north-east of the centre of Leeds, and is on the A58 Leeds to Wetherby road. Turn left off the A58 into the village centre and continue past the church to the Bingley Arms. Alternatively, there is an hourly bus service from Leeds along the A58.

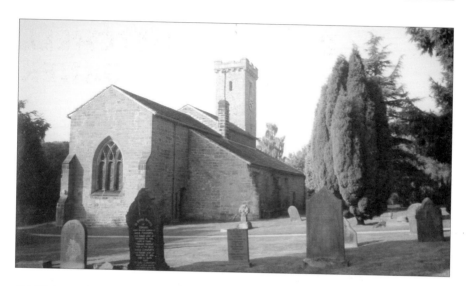

ALL HALLOWS CHURCH, BARDSEY

*B*etween Leeds and Wetherby, and no more than a few miles from the centre of Leeds, is some attractive walking country. It doesn't have the spectacular topography that you marvel at in the Pennines. Instead, it is a well-wooded landscape of low hills and steep valleys, more reminiscent of Hertfordshire than Yorkshire. There are no spectacular vistas that stretch for miles and miles, but there are many charming small-scale views. Much of the walk is on the magnesium limestone belt; the rock doesn't outcrop on the walk, but it is the building stone of virtually all of the older houses in and around Thorner. To the west of the limestone belt is a coarse sandstone and this forms the surprise crags that pop up through the trees at Hetchell.

This isn't a flat walk by any stretch of the imagination, and some of the ups and downs are quite steep; however, none of them is prolonged. The most common bird you are likely to see is the pheasant, and, of the domestic animals, horses are probably more numerous than cows. It is a walk that is best done in April or May when the leaves are just coming out, but those who have a predilection for autumn colour will find it a cheap and convenient alternative to New England.

The **Bingley Arms**, which traces its history back to 905, claims to be the oldest pub in England, and has priest holes and a secret passageway. It offers a wide range of tempting main courses and these include pasta dishes, traditional pie of the day, and curry of the day. The real ales are Black Sheep, Taylor's Landlord, and Tetley's. Food is available from Tuesday to Friday from noon to 2.30 pm and from 6 pm to 9.30 pm; on Saturdays from noon to 9.30 pm; and on Sundays from noon to 7 pm. The pub is closed on Mondays. Telephone: 01937 574280.

Bardsey is a neat and tidy commuter village. Its steep hillsides and tree-lined lanes give it a particular charm. As well as an ancient pub, it has an ancient church, All Hallows, with a tower that dates back to Saxon times and is also well worth a visit.

① From the Bingley Arms, turn right along the main street to the **church of All Hallows**. Continue along the street until you reach the main A58. Go right for 100 yards, and then turn left through some iron posts and into a wood. (If construction work is still in progress, it may be necessary to turn into the wood earlier.) Diagonally cross the old railway line (formerly the Leeds to Wetherby and Harrogate route) and continue along the path through attractive woodland, thereafter keeping to the bottom edge of the fields close to a wooded valley. The path enters **Hetchell Wood**, a nature reserve, through a gap in the fence, and continues in the same direction, never far away from the stream on the right. **Hetchell Crags** are high up on the left near the end of the wood.

② Turn left when the path comes to a lane beside a footbridge, and climb gently, with Hetchell Wood on the left; you are now at **Pompocali**. Cross the metalled road and make your way to a well-defined bridle path on the right-hand side of a field. You are now on a Roman road, but not for long, as the path, still close to the hedge, soon swings round to the right and then enters a wood, following its left-hand edge for some distance.

③ Turn right when you come to a T-junction at the end of the wood; then almost immediately turn left along an attractive green lane. This enters another wood, **Ragdale Plantation**, and keeps to its left-hand edge. Go right where the path divides; it swings gradually right, with a stream, **Milnes Beck**, close by on the left. The mixed woodland and easy path provide very enjoyable walking. When the path comes into a field, turn right and keep close to the hedge as you gradually climb the hillside.

④ At the top of the hill, turn left onto **Kennels Lane**, and follow this for half a mile. It is a pleasant, quiet lane with high hedges on both sides. Over the hedge to the right, the thundering hoofs of racehorses can sometimes be heard. Turn left at the signpost for 'public footpath **Thorner** via **Jubilee Bridge'**. There are good views from this point.

Follow the path down the field, with the hedge on the right, and carry straight on into the woodland. The path crosses the stream on **Jubilee Bridge**, which is a substantial wooden structure, and swings right for a few yards and then left to a stile into a meadow. The clear path now lies half-way up the hillside in attractive surroundings, going over a stile and crossing another field to a kissing gate just to the left of a large tree stump. Turn left along the metalled road and you will soon see the tower of **Thorner church** straight ahead.

THE BINGLEY ARMS DATES BACK TO THE 10TH CENTURY

THE FORD AT THORNER

⑤ Turn right at the road junction and go along the main street of **Thorner**. You can walk inside the churchyard for a few yards. (Parts of the church date back to the 14th century.) Continue along the main street, a pleasant wide village street with many attractive houses in local stone, and at its end turn right over a footbridge by the ford. There is a convenient seat if you want to sit down and enjoy the scene. Go along the lane, past houses, to a footpath sign, and continue in the same direction, keeping close to a hedge on the right. (There is a good view from the top of the field.) Go over the stile by the footpath sign, down a short field, and then briefly left after the stile. In a few yards, the path turns right and keeps along the hedge for a couple of fields before turning sharp right to a metalled road.

⑥ Go left along the road, and after a short distance turn right through some stone gateposts marked '**Eltofts House** private entrance'. Keep along the metalled drive until a row of houses is reached on the right (another good viewpoint). Go over the stile opposite the houses and follow a clear path along the side of the valley. The path then enters **Kidhirst Wood** and gradually descends through fine beeches to a lake. Continue past another conveniently placed seat, and then turn up a wide track on the right.

Ignore the stile into the field, but veer left and keep in the wood. About 100 yards after the track emerges onto a lane, turn left through a waymarked metal gate. The path goes through another gate and then steeply down a meadow to a stile by a signpost. Turn left along the metalled road for about a quarter of a mile until you reach a house on the right.

⑦ Turn right down a lane signed '**Leeds Country Way**', which you remain on for the rest of the walk. After a few yards, go over a stile on the left, and follow the path by the hedge to a stile, and then a footbridge over a stream. The path now bends left and goes along an overgrown green lane. (Note the fishponds through the hedge on the left.) When you come into a field, turn right by the hedge. The path goes over the top of a hill and down the other side to a signpost. Turn left along the bottom of the field to reach the A58 again.

⑧ Go left for a few yards, and then turn right along an unsurfaced road with houses on the right, **Wayside Gardens**. Keep straight on along the lane after the end of the houses. When you come to more houses, go into the field (another good viewpoint) and continue in the same direction by the hedge on the left. Towards the bottom of the field, the path slants right and goes through trees to a gate into **Bardsey churchyard**. Go through the churchyard to Bardsey's main street, an attractive finish to the walk.

Date walk completed:

ADDINGHAM TO BOLTON ABBEY AND BEAMSLEY BEACON

THE RUINS OF BOLTON PRIORY

Distance:
10 miles

Starting Point:
The Fleece pub,
Addingham.
GR 078497

Map: OS Explorer 27, Lower Wharfedale and Washburn Valley

How to get there: Addingham is just in West Yorkshire, 3 miles west of Ilkley. Go along the main A65 from Ilkley, and then turn right into Addingham. The Fleece is the first pub on the right on Main Street, which runs right through the middle of the village.

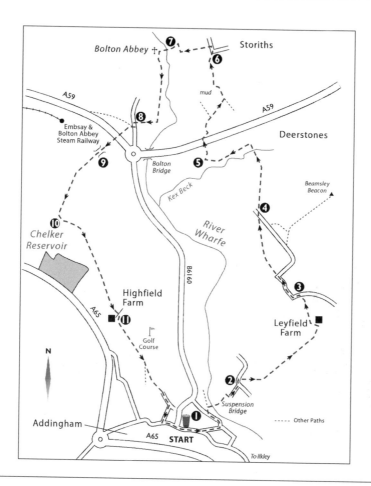

*B*olton Abbey is a place of great beauty and considerable historical interest, and the walk approaches it by the best of all routes, down the path from Storiths. Another highlight of the walk is Kex Beck, a gem of a secret valley. Much of the walk is on lightly trodden paths in an attractive Wharfedale landscape of pasture, moorland, and wooded vales. The shapely Beamsley Beacon (1,245 ft) dominates the scene throughout, and the energetic can extend the walk by climbing it. An extension for the less energetic is a train ride with real steam engines.

The Fleece, which dates back to 1740, is popular both with local people and visitors. It has an extensive blackboard and weekly specials, including a wide range of meat and fish courses. Popular choices include meat and potato pie, Wharfedale game pie, wok fried king prawns, with garlic and lemon, and braised shoulder of lamb. Opening times are from noon to 11 pm (10.30 pm on Sundays). Last orders for food are 2.15 pm for lunch and 9.15 pm for dinner. On Sundays food is served from noon to 8 pm. The real ales are Black Sheep, Tetley, and Timothy Taylor. Telephone: 01943 830491.

The Walk

Addingham is a large village strung along a winding main street of considerable length; in fact it used to be called Long Addingham. It was formerly a textile village and had handloom weavers' cottages, loom shops, and five mills. Not many years ago the main street was the busy A65 between Leeds and the Yorkshire Dales, but the village has now been bypassed and is a rather quieter place.

① Turn left after leaving the **Fleece**, walk down the main street, and turn left along **Church Street**. At the T-junction, turn left along **North Street** (note the interesting display board about Addingham), then take the **Dalesway** path on the right. Then, disregard the **Dalesway**, and instead cross the suspension bridge over the **River Wharfe**. Continue along a tarmac path to the end of the field, and then go over a footbridge and through a gate and turn left up the farm access road.

② Turn left at the road junction, and then almost immediately go over a stile on the right. Cross the large field to a stile near the top right-hand corner; then climb steadily up the side of the next field, ignoring the path into the wood. The path eventually enters the wood after a stone stile and goes beside a ravine. Beyond the wood, continue up the field towards **Leyfield Farm**, and go over a stile on the left. Keep close to the fence on the right and go over a stone stile; cross the field to a yellow post, and then descend steeply into a small wooded valley. Negotiate the contortionist stile at the other side, and cross the field to the left of a bungalow. Turn left past some abandoned vehicles, and follow an overgrown path between farm buildings and a wall to reach a road.

③ Turn left along the road as far as a sharp right-hand bend after a quarter of a mile. Leave the road here and cross a small pocket of unfenced grassland to a stile to the right of a cattle grid. Follow an attractive path through a wood and across several meadows before coming into open moorland with excellent views of Wharfedale straight ahead. Cross the metalled road to a footpath sign for **Ling Chapel**.

(Those who want to extend the walk to **Beamsley Beacon** should keep going along the road after the right-hand bend, and then turn off at the footpath sign and climb up to the trig point. On the descent, retrace your steps to the road, and then turn right to the **Ling Chapel** sign – a short cut goes by the wall on the right just before the bottom of the descent.)

④ Go along the moorland path to **Ling Chapel** and make for the signpost to the left of the farm. Take the path signed 'Deerstones' down to the attractive wooded valley of **Kex Beck**. (Note: this path, though signed, is not marked on the Explorer map; it is an unclassified county road.) The path crosses the beck by a wooden bridge, and then zigzags up the hillside to **Deerstones**. Turn left at the first

THE FLEECE, AT ADDINGHAM

house and follow a delightful path down the valley, at first in woodland and then in fields. When the second field narrows, turn right up an indistinct track through gorse bushes to a stile by a gate, and continue by the wall on the left to the A59 road from Harrogate to Skipton.

⑤ Cross the road with extreme care, and go up the path by the postbox. At the footpath signpost, turn left along an access road that goes between buildings and then into a field. Where the road turns left, continue in the same direction to a gate; then keep along the valley to a step stile. Veer left up the hill in the next field to a gate by a footpath signpost; then go left along a wall and follow the path across fields to a ladder stile over a wall. Slant left and cross a muddy rivulet – there are helpful stones if you look carefully – to a step stile. The well-signed path now hugs the wall on the right for two fields, and then turns right to the hamlet of **Storiths**.

⑥ Go straight ahead on a lane into a farmyard, left through a farmgate, and then through a smaller gate into a narrow walled lane. This is a beautiful part of the walk, with glimpses of **Bolton Abbey** straight ahead and moorland views to the right. Beyond the lane, descend through mature woodland to the **River Wharfe**, which the more

adventurous can cross by the stepping stones instead of the footbridge.

In front of you is Bolton Abbey, more accurately Bolton Priory, in a beautiful setting. It was originally a monastery, founded by the Augustinian canons in the 12th century. After the dissolution of the monasteries by Henry VIII, the eastern part of the building gradually fell into ruin. The western part, however, became the local parish church, and is a fine example of early Gothic architecture.

⑦ On leaving the abbey, go along the riverside path down the valley towards the graceful stone arches of **Bolton Bridge**. Turn right after a kissing gate, and continue along a fence to the **Devonshire Arms** car park.

⑧ Take the bridleway opposite the hotel (formerly the main road to Skipton). After a few yards, go over a stile on the left – a real de luxe job! – then over a footbridge, and up to a stile onto the A59. Cross the road to another stile, and then continue up the side of the field and over a stone railway bridge. Deep below is the former Ilkley to Skipton line.

(If you want to take a ride on the **Embsay and Bolton Abbey Steam Railway**, ignore the de luxe stile and continue along the bridleway until it reaches the A59; then turn right for a few yards to the station.)

⑨ Continue then up the field by the wall on the right. There are good views of **Simon's Seat**, more or less behind you, and to the left **Beamsley Beacon** and **Ilkley Moor**. Go through the gate at the top of the field, and continue in the same direction to a stile over a fence. In the next field, keep to the right of the hill, **Haw Pike**, and make for the clump of trees on the horizon. Then swing left of the trees, through a gate to the right of a house, and down the access road.

⑩ Immediately after the access road joins a road from the nearby farm, strike left through a plantation of young trees and go over a wooden stile. The path climbs steeply up the left side of the field to a step stile requiring acrobatic skills and a cool head. Now keep close to the wall on your left; go over a stile by the gate, and in the next field keep by the wall on the right. The path then goes through the right-hand one of the two gates and keeps to the wall on the left again. When level with the wind turbine, cross the wall by a step stile. Go straight on for a few yards, turn right through a gate, and follow the wall on your right. Cross the wall

by a step stile, turn left along it to a gate, and then cross the field in the direction of **Highfield Farm**, to a stone step stile close to a bank. Make for a gate beside a tree just to the left of the farmhouse, and follow the waymarked path round the buildings. Still in the farmyard, turn left immediately after a low brick building and go through a gate. Now go straight ahead across the field and over a stile by the gate, ignoring the step stile further to the right.

⑪ Continue in the same direction across **Bracken Ghyll Golf Course**, following the line of white and green posts. If you hear shouts of 'Fore!', duck immediately with your arms over your head. The path leaves the golf course and enters an avenue of mature hawthorns. Take the left-hand one of the two waymarked options, and continue downhill, always keeping close to the wooded banks of a sunken lane on the left. The path eventually joins the lane, which soon leads into **Addingham**. Turn right along the metalled road, **Chapel Street**, and continue past the former Wesleyan Methodist chapel (built in 1778, and now apartments) to Addingham's main street. The **Fleece** is a few pubs further down on the left.

Date walk completed:

SUTTON-IN-CRAVEN, SLIPPERY FORD AND THE PINNACLES

LOOKING TOWARDS WAINMAN'S PINNACLE AND PENDLE HILL

Distance:
12 miles

Starting Point:
The church at
Sutton-in-Craven.
GR 007442

Map: OS Outdoor Leisure 21 South Pennines

How to get there: *From Keighley, go along the A629 towards Skipton, and at the end of the dual carriageway take the A6068 towards Colne. Turn left in the middle of Cross Hills onto the road signed to Sutton (the signpost is on the side of a building and the turn is immediately after a pelican crossing). Turn left opposite the Black Bull and park nearby.*

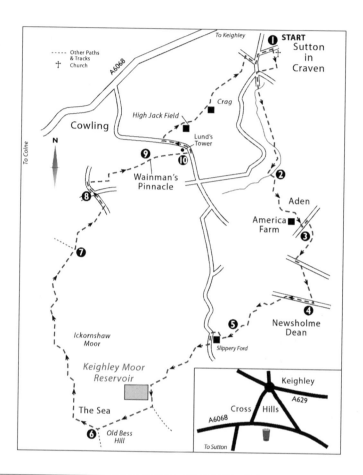

This is a splendid upland walk on the Pennine hills just west of Keighley. The path from Sutton-in-Craven leads straight into a different world with a steep-sided, wooded valley and a fast flowing stream. The route then climbs to a landscape of upland pasture before dropping into the upper part of the valley that leads to Slippery Ford. The next part of the route is on moorland with extensive views. The conspicuous towers on Earl Crag, known as the Pinnacles, are visited on the return journey. Much of the walk is on lightly used paths: keep using them!

The Old White Bear is on the A6068 in Cross Hills. It dates back to 1735. A very recent claim to fame is that it brews its own beer, which is deservedly popular. There are bar meals, including a home-made steak in ale pie, and a variety of main courses, such as duck with cherries, are available in the restaurant. Meals are available from noon to 2.30 pm from Tuesday to Sunday, and from 6 pm to 9 pm from Tuesday to Saturday. Real ales are Old Bear Original (brewed on the premises), Boddingtons, and Old Speckled Hen. Telephone: 01535 632115.

The Walk

Sutton-in-Craven is a former mill village, and Greenroyd Mill, the large building which still dominates the top end of the village, employed over 200 people shortly before its closure in 1980.

① Park in the village near the church. Walk up the lane between the church and the school, and turn right at the T-junction along a path that soon leads onto a road at the southern end of the village. Turn right, then immediately left, and left again, by a wooden seat inscribed 'Sutton Conservation Group 1997 rest your ass a while'. Go up the lane and beneath the imposing archway.

This fine stone archway graces the former drive to Sutton Hall (now demolished), which was once the home of John William Hartley, whose family owned

Greenroyd Mill. The Hartley trademark is visible on the centre of the arch.

The lane crosses **Sutton Beck** by a footbridge and enters a deep, wooded valley. Follow the broad track up the valley on the left-hand side of the stream. When the broad track comes to an end, turn right and cross the footbridge over the stream. (Note: there is more than one bridge – make sure you don't go over a bridge too soon!) The path now keeps fairly close to the stream and then climbs steeply through rocks, to divide just after passing between two large rocks. Ignore the path that climbs steeply up the side of the valley, and take the one, faint at first, which fords the stream and winds up the other side of the valley to a stile at the top of the wood.

② Go to the right across the field to a stile on the left-hand side of the house, and continue through the garden and out into another field, keeping the wall on your left. Turn right near the bottom, cross a difficult stile, and descend to a bridge over the stream. Almost immediately, the path goes over a scarcely discernible stile on the left. Keep close to the wall in the next two fields, and then go through a gate into a green lane. Go along the lane past the ducks and then through a gate into the farmyard at **Aden**. Immediately after the farmhouse, slant to the right across the field to a gate in the far corner. Now turn right and go up to **America Farm**. (Aden to America in ten minutes!) Go between the two houses, and then carry straight on up the hill to **America Lane**.

③ Turn left for about 100 yards; then go over a stile at the top of a bank on the right. Make for the gate in the right-hand top corner of the field. You are now on top of the world in an attractive upland landscape of green fields and brown walls. (Look back for a good view of **Airedale** and **Ilkley Moor**.) Once through the gate, go almost immediately through another one; then the route is more or less in the same direction through gates and stiles to a metalled road. The small hill on the left is **Pole Stoop**. Turn left along the road, and then go along the second footpath on the

LUND'S TOWER

right, which is about 100 yards after the first path and just before an isolated hawthorn bush. Now continue across several fields, keeping close to a wall on the right.

④ Turn right when the path comes to **Todley Hall Road**, and then go down the second lane on the left, marked '**Bottoms Farm**'. The waymarked path goes round to the right of the house, and over a stile into a field of rough pasture. There are fine views down the wooded valley of **Newsholme Dean**. The clearly waymarked route goes through gates and stiles, before turning left and dropping down to a ford. (Note that this waymarked route is well to the left of the path marked on the Outdoor Leisure map.) I do not know whether the ford is the real Slippery Ford, but it is certainly a very pleasant spot.

⑤ After the ford, keep to the left of the field; then go through a gate and into the farmyard at **Slippery Ford**. Turn left down the metalled road; then go through a gate on the right and follow the road up the moor to **Keighley Moor Reservoir**. Go across the dam, and take the permissive path to the right, which goes across moorland for half a mile before meeting the Pennine Way at **Old Bess Hill**.

⑥ Turn right along the **Pennine Way** on a fine moorland path, and

veer right after a third of a mile by a sheep feeding trough at **The Sea**. The path goes over the crest of the moor, well to the right of the trig point on Wolf Stones. (The views are extensive in all directions, and on the left **Pendle Hill** (1,764 ft) is particularly prominent. Its steep northern face makes it one of the most distinctive peaks in the Pennines.) The path gradually descends to a stone shooting lodge and then keeps by a wall on the left, passing several huts with chimneys, which have been there for decades and blend into the landscape.

⑦ After going over a ladder stile, do not turn left along the **Pennine Way** but go straight on for a few yards and then through a stile in the wall on the right. There is no clear path, but keep close to the wall as you descend to the next field. Then slant right and cross a very marshy meadow to a footbridge at the bottom of a steep-sided valley. Go over a stile, cross a small stream by a stone slab, and then make for the gate to the right of the house at the top of the field. Go down the drive of the house and turn left along the metalled lane.

⑧ Keep straight on at the crossroads and go down **Old Lane**. At the first house on the right, go on the path between the buildings and continue across a field, keeping close to the wall on the left. Turn left along a muddy green lane for a few yards; then turn right immediately after the gate and climb steeply by a wall on the right. Continue in the same direction across fields and go to the immediate left of the farm buildings at **Hallan Hill**; then climb gently across moorland to **Wainman's Pinnacle**, a slender stone tower with a pointed top.

⑨ Continue on an airy path along the top of **Earl Crag** to **Lund's Tower**, the second of the two pinnacles that grace the gritstone edge.

The view from Lund's Tower is outstanding and includes Pendle Hill, Ingleborough (always a stirring sight), Penyghent, Buckden Pike, Simon's Seat, and Beamsley Beacon. You can climb the tower by a dark spiral staircase, and then sit amongst the crenellations to admire the prospect.

⑩ Go down the steep path to the road, and turn left. There are good views of the edge you have walked along. After a quarter of a mile, turn sharp right through a gate along a farm track which goes just to the right of a house and gradually descends to **High Jack Field**. Keep straight on by the left of the house, through a gate at the end of the garden, and into a field. Keep close to the fence on the left, and then, immediately after two large sycamore trees, go through a stile by a gate. Slant across the field down to a stile at the bottom corner, and then go over another stile just to the left of the house at **Crag** (the dogs are on a lead!). Turn left down the access road, and when it splits into two take the lane to the right, which soon leads into **Sutton-in-Craven**. Turn right when you get into the village, and then left at the **King's Arms**. After a few yards, you will be back where the walk started. To get to the **Old White Bear**, go back along the road to **Cross Hills** and turn right at the T-junction along the A6068 towards **Keighley**. The pub is on the right after 200 yards.

Date walk completed:

CARLETON, CARLETON GLEN AND PINHAW

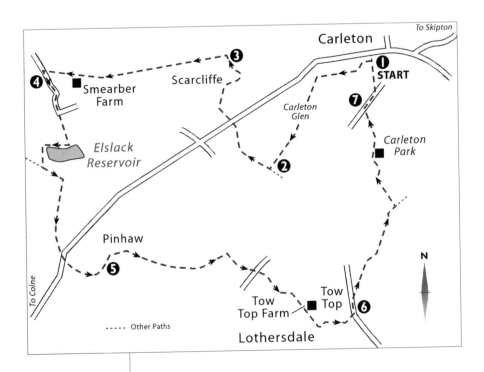

Distance:
10 miles

Starting Point:
The main road junction in the middle of Carleton. Park in the village.
GR 973497

Map: OS Outdoor Leisure 21 South Pennines

How to get there: *Carleton is 2 miles south-west of Skipton. Approach Skipton by the A629 from Keighley. Leave the A629 at the roundabout and take the A6131 towards the town centre. Immediately after going under a railway bridge, turn left to Carleton at traffic lights. There is a frequent rail service from Leeds and Bradford to Skipton.*

ON THE OUTSKIRTS OF CARLETON

This is a splendid and varied walk in a little known part of Airedale. The first part of the route goes up the secret valley of Carleton Glen. It then climbs Pinhaw, which is not only a delightful heather-strewn hill, but one of the best viewpoints in the Pennines, and, on a clear day, the Lake District hills can easily be seen from it. On the return section of the walk there are fine views into Lothersdale and Airedale.

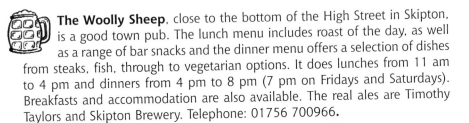

The Woolly Sheep, close to the bottom of the High Street in Skipton, is a good town pub. The lunch menu includes roast of the day, as well as a range of bar snacks and the dinner menu offers a selection of dishes from steaks, fish, through to vegetarian options. It does lunches from 11 am to 4 pm and dinners from 4 pm to 8 pm (7 pm on Fridays and Saturdays). Breakfasts and accommodation are also available. The real ales are Timothy Taylors and Skipton Brewery. Telephone: 01756 700966.

The Walk

Carleton is a former mill village, attractively sited at the foot of the hills. The mill has now been converted to apartments. Nearby Skipton is a town of character, with a busy market, a castle, and interesting churches. It has been a market town since the 13th century. Its charm is enhanced by the Leeds and Liverpool Canal that winds through its centre.

① From the road junction in the middle of **Carleton**, take the road westwards towards **Colne** in **Lancashire**. After 100 yards or so, just before the road crosses a stream, turn left on a footpath beside a wall. The path climbs steeply and, just before a flight of steps, take the path that veers to the right through woodland and then back to the stream. Turn left when it comes to a lane, and continue past farm buildings and up the valley; you are now at the beginning of **Carleton Glen**. The lane, now unfenced, climbs the glen through attractive meadows and ends at a gate; here you swing to the left along a path marked by white posts, which keeps close to a wooded gorge before descending to a stile and crossing a stream. Go up the steep bank straight ahead, and then turn left, keeping close to the edge of a wooded valley. On your right is a grass-covered earthwork, roughly circular in form. At the top of the field is a stile designed for very slim people, or you can use the nearby gate instead. Now climb the field to a gate in the far right corner; then keep close to the fence on the right as it leads down to a stream. Cross the stream as best you can – the stepping stones marked on the map are an exaggeration – and then go over an awkward stile a few yards upstream. Climb up the steep bank and then turn left up the field to a step stile over the wall. Continue up the next field to a stile in front of the farmhouse.

② Turn right along the farm access road, with good views to the right. Turn left when you come to a more substantial road (the road to **Colne** again), and then in a short while turn right through a narrow gate onto a moor. The path keeps close to the wall, but after 200 yards or so veers right along a shallow depression and then swings right again, passing a house on the left, **Higher Scarcliff**. Immediately after passing the second house, **Lower Scarcliff**, turn sharp left along a farm road which crosses a field to a cattle grid.

③ In following the path for the next mile, the main thing to bear in mind is that it goes in an almost straight line, but sometimes it is on one side of the wall and sometimes on the other. Turn left off the farm road immediately after the grid and climb gently up the field, keeping close to the wall on the left. Go through the gate just before **Yellison Wood**, and now walk along the attractive moorland path, with the wall on your right. Go over a stile, and then go through the second gate on the right. Walk through fields, keeping the wall on your left, and continue in the same direction across the open field to an awkward step stile just left of where the wall juts out. Through the next

SKIPTON

two fields the wall is on your right again, and then you go through a gate beside an oak tree. Veer slightly right across the next field to a stile in front of **Smearber Farm**; then go through the farmyard and down a pleasant lane to a T-junction.

④ Turn left up the metalled road for about a quarter of a mile to where the road bends left at **Stories House**. Go through the stile on the right by the footpath sign; then immediately after go through the gate on the left and up to the access road to **Elslack Reservoir**. Where the road divides, take the right-hand option, which winds round the dam of the reservoir. Then continue through a gate into the conifer wood, and at the T-junction of tracks turn left. Watch carefully for a waymark on a tree stump on the right after about 200 yards, and turn right up a steep path, indistinct at first, into the woodland. It soon leads into a field, and the path keeps in the same direction by the wall as it climbs up the hillside. Go over another difficult stile by a gate at the top of the field; then the path, still climbing, veers slightly right across **Elslack Moor**, with impressive views to the right. Turn right for a few yards when you come to the road (the **Colne road** again), and then left along the **Pennine Way** as it gently climbs to the top of **Pinhaw**.

On a warm day the heather-clad top of Pinhaw is a pleasant spot to linger, and the views are outstanding. To the south-west is Boulsworth Hill, and round to the west Weets Top (just beyond Barnoldswick) and Pendle Hill dominate the scene. Further round towards the north, the distinctive stepped shape of Ingleborough is dominant on a clear day, and if you are really lucky you will be able to see the Lakeland fells. To the north-east, Simon's Seat can be seen, and then to the right of this is Beamsley Beacon, backed by Round Hill. To the south-east is a good view of Airedale, and you will also be able to clearly see the two pinnacles above Cowling. The attractive green valley at your feet to the south is Lothersdale.

⑤ When you eventually decide to leave the top, continue along the **Pennine Way** as you gradually descend, still with good views of **Lothersdale**. The path turns to the right as it comes off the moor, and then shortly afterwards crosses a metalled road. In the second field after the road, part company with the **Pennine Way** and keep fairly close to the wall on the left. The path is indistinct, but the line you want is the farm on the hillside, **Tow Top Farm**. The path eventually goes into a walled green lane, which drops to a stream and then climbs up the hillside past the farm and swings round to the left. Almost immediately, go over a fine stone step stile on the right, and then go down the field, keeping close to the wall. Do not go through the gate straight ahead, but turn left along the wall to a stile by a footpath sign.

⑥ Turn left up the metalled road for a few hundred yards, and then go over the stile beside the farm access road to **Tow Top**. The path keeps the wall on the right for three fields. In the next field, go to the left of a wind-battered oak to a stile in the field corner. The path keeps close to the wall on the right in the next field as it skirts **Burnt Hill**. There are fine views across **Airedale**. In the next field the path swings right and descends to a shallow hollow at the beginning of a ridge. Turn left through a metal gate here and go straight down the side of the moor, keeping the wall on your left. The strange wooden contraption to the right of the path is probably a grouse butt. At the bottom of the hill, go over a stile, and then cross the field towards the left of the

farm, **Carleton Park**. Go through a gate and across the farm access road, and then go through the left-hand one of the two gates straight ahead. Keep to the wall on your right for a while before slanting across to a stile at the far left corner of the field. In the next field, veer left to a step stile over the wall, and then turn right alongside the wall to a stile at the bottom. Turn left and almost immediately you come to **Park Lane**.

⑦ Turn right and go down the tree-lined lane. After about 300 yards and immediately before a seat, go over a stile on the left and into a field. Slant across to the right and savour the stunning view over **Carleton**, dominated by the the tall stone chimney of the former mill. Descend the steep hillside to a passage between the bungalows at the bottom. Keep straight on, and go down the steps into the wood where the walk started. At the bottom of the wood turn right for the village centre.

Date walk completed:

WASHBURN VALLEY WALK: SWINSTY RESERVOIR, LINDLEY WOOD AND DOBPARK BRIDGE

DOBPARK BRIDGE

Distance:
12 miles

Starting Point:
Yorkshire Water car park on the eastern side of Swinsty Reservoir. GR 198535

Map: OS Explorer 27, Lower Wharfedale and Washburn Valley

How to get there: *Take the B6451 north from Otley. After about 5 miles along an attractive road with good views, turn left down Smithson's Lane, signed 'Fewston'. The car park for the start of the walk is on the left, just after an arm of the reservoir is crossed. The Sun Inn is a few hundred yards further along the B6451 after the Fewston turn.*

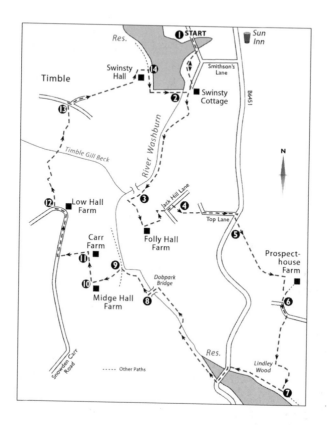

As well as its beauty, the Washburn Valley has another great asset: a dense network of attractive footpaths and bridleways, which is made full use of in this walk. Most of the walk is on paths that are fairly well trodden, but, in order to take in some of the best views and most attractive paths, the route is quite intricate. A good time of the year to do this walk is April, particularly late April, when there is a full range of spring flowers. You will see violets, primroses, wood anemones, bluebells, celandines, and marsh marigolds in profusion, and the gorse will still be in full flush. Before you start the walk, find time to look at Yorkshire Water's noticeboard display on the Washburn Valley reservoirs.

The **Sun Inn** is a friendly, unpretentious pub, popular with walkers, families, and bikers. It serves food most of the day, apart from a two hour break in the late afternoon. There is a carvery with a choice of meats, and one, two, or three course meals are available, as well as burger and chips. The real ale is Theakstone and Old Speckled Hen, plus a guest beer, which was Ridley's on my visit. Telephone: 01943 880220.

① From the car park, turn right and walk back along **Smithson's Lane** across an inlet of the reservoir. Then immediately turn right through a gate to follow the permissive path and then a metalled road alongside the reservoir.

② Immediately after **Swinsty Cottage**, and before the road turns onto the embankment, go through a gate on the left. Turn sharp left towards a plantation of pines, and then slant down the hillside to a stile in the bottom of the valley. Continue along the valley, with the **River Washburn** on your right. The well-wooded banks are full of flowers in spring.

I'm very fond of the Washburn Valley; it is beautiful and sparsely populated. It's not much visited, even by walkers, although the lower end of the valley is no more than a few miles from the million or more people who live in nearby Leeds and Bradford. Like most

Pennine valleys, the Washburn Valley is steep-sided and well wooded. It also has four large and attractive reservoirs providing water for Leeds. The reservoirs of course have been the key factor in keeping the more visible forms of urbanization out of the valley. Before they were built, however, the valley was a busy industrial area, and in the upper part there were several linen mills, whose overgrown sites can still be traced.

③ After a gate and a wide bridge over the **Washburn** on the right, immediately slant left (by concrete water signs marked 'AV') through woodland and up a farm track to **Folly Hall Farm**. Go through the farm buildings and round to the left up a lane which climbs quite steeply. Turn left along a lane by a footpath sign, and then almost immediately turn right. In a few yards turn left up **Jack Hill Lane**.

④ A few yards up the lane, bear right through a snicket stile. The path, which becomes sunken, climbs through banks of gorse, aglow with colour in early spring. Keep climbing and ignore the stile into the wood on the right. Go over the ladder stile near the corner of the walls, and continue through three fields.

There are fine views to the left over Swinsty Reservoir to the upper Washburn Valley, and further round the big white balls (actually radar discs) of the U.S. intelligence-gathering station at Menwith Hill dominate the scene.

When the path comes to **Top Lane**, continue in the same direction (due east).

To the right, after the end of the wood, there are good views across the lower Washburn Valley. The ruins of Dobpark Lodge, a former hunting lodge, can be seen at the far side of the valley, and, further afield, the edge of Ilkley Moor.

⑤ At the end of Top Lane, cross the busy B6451 – taking care, as you are at the crest of a hill – and enter **Norwood Edge Plantation** by the footpath sign. Continue along the path in a south-easterly direction, ignoring the forest road that veers to the left. At the end of the wood, keep going in the same direction

THE SUN INN, NEAR SWINSTY RESERVOIR

across a boggy meadow towards **Prospecthouse Farm**. Go through a farm gate and, almost immediately after, go through another farm gate on the right. Go straight across the field and through the gate at the bottom; then go down the farm road to a metalled road.

⑥ Turn left along the road, and then go right along a lane marked '**Wood Top Farm**'. The lane becomes a farm track and goes through several fields with splendid views over to **Otley Chevin**, **Ilkley Moor**, and the hills beyond **Queensbury**. In the last field before **Lindley Wood**, the wall turns sharp left and the path follows it to a stile into the wood, which is full of bluebells in spring. The path descends steeply to **Lindley Wood Reservoir**.

⑦ Turn right along a well-used path until the B6451 is reached again. Turn left along the road across the reservoir, and go through a stile on the right. The path goes along the top end of the reservoir (good for aquatic birdlife, including herons), and then through meadows up the valley, crossing the **Washburn** on a stone bridge en route. The path comes to a lane, and almost immediately you come to **Dobpark Bridge**, a fine packhorse bridge and one of the gems of the valley. This is a good place to stop and savour the scene for a few minutes.

⑧ Suitably refreshed, go over the stile on the right at the far side of the bridge and up the valley through woodland, with the river close by. The path then goes through three fields, still with the river not far away on the right, before reaching further woodland.

⑨ As you enter the wood, a small stream is crossed, and then you leave the main path to go through a gate on the left. There are two footpaths at this point, and you want the right-hand one that goes through a gate close to the deep ravine of **Snowden Beck**. Continue upwards on a path through woodland full of hollies and carpeted with bluebells, ignoring a path that crosses the ravine. The path emerges on a narrow, walled lane, with **Midge Hall Farm** on the left.

⑩ At the T-junction turn right onto a green lane. Continue through meadows to farm buildings immediately on your left, with **Carr Farm** on the right.

⑪ Turn left up the farm road, and then turn right at the top, along **Snowden Carr Road**, which is metalled.

This is another good viewpoint; the wooded ridge along which Top Lane runs is particularly prominent.

⑫ Just after **Snowden Carr Road** bends sharp left, go right, and take the left one of two lanes, making sure you keep Manor House on your right. Follow this lane, another of the gems of the **Washburn Valley**, for about a mile towards **Timble**. When the lane, now entirely green, turns right and emerges into an open field, go sharp left along the line of an old wall, to reach a gate into a narrow lane at the far side. The lane and **Dick's Beck** soon become more or less the same thing, but the good news is that it is solid beneath the shallow stream. Ignore the stile on the left, and continue along the stream bed. The lane then fords **Timble Gill Beck** and climbs steadily towards **Timble**.

⑬ At the top of the lane, turn right along the metalled lane (there are fine views down the valley), and then almost immediately bear left along a grassy lane. The path then continues in the same direction across several fields; aim for the gates and you will find a stile at the side. In the field before **Swinsty Moor Plantation**, make for the blue Yorkshire Water noticeboard. Continue in the same direction in the wood; then veer left along a permissive path. Turn sharp right to a gate close to **Swinsty Hall**, an attractive Elizabethan building, and then go down a gravel road.

⑭ When the well-used lane beside **Swinsty Reservoir** is reached, turn right. The lane leads to the reservoir embankment, where there are fine views on either side, and then comes to **Swinsty Cottage**, which was passed in the early part of the walk. From here, retrace your steps along the side of the reservoir to the car park.

Now drive back up **Smithson's Lane** to the B6451, turn left, and very soon you will come to the **Sun Inn**.

Date walk completed:

NIDDERDALE WALK: PATELEY BRIDGE, GUISECLIFF, FOSSE GILL AND MOSSCAR BOTTOM

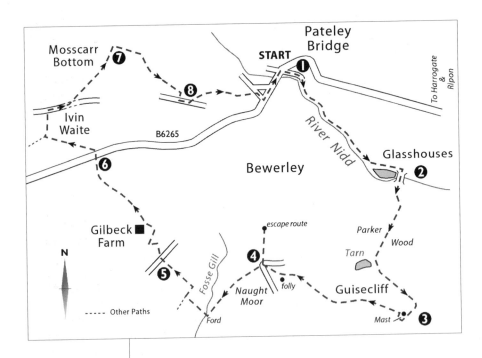

Distance:
9 Miles

Starting Point:
The riverside car park at Pateley Bridge.
GR 158655

Map: OS Explorer 26, Nidderdale

How to get there: *Turn left off the A61 Harrogate–Ripon road at Ripley, and take the B6165/B6265 up the Nidd valley to Pateley Bridge. At the bottom of Pateley Bridge High Street and immediately before the bridge over the Nidd, turn left to the riverside car park, 300 yards along the road. At the time of writing, all-day parking was £1.*

GUISECLIFF AND NIDDERDALE

*N*idderdale is perhaps the most underrated of the major Yorkshire Dales, perhaps because it is not in the Yorkshire Dales National Park. The Nidd starts on Great Whernside, one of Yorkshire's highest hills (2,230 ft), soon becomes engulfed in large reservoirs built to supply Bradford, and then makes its way south-eastwards through Nidderdale along a deep, well-wooded valley, which we follow in the early part of the walk. We pass a tarn before coming to Guisecliff, one of Yorkshire's best edges, and the path along the top provides exhilarating walking with fine views. There are notices warning of dangerous crevasses and some big drops over the cliff too so great care needs to be taken here. Then comes the real challenge of this adventurous walk: the ford over Fosse Gill. In dry times you are unlikely to get your feet wet, but the last time I tackled it was after an 'unsettled' few days, and Fosse Gill was running above ankle height; so I took off my boots and socks and waded across. It is likely to be at least this high throughout the winter, so I recommend this as a summer only walk, although there is an escape route if the gill is impassable. The return leg of this glorious walk is on infrequently used paths.

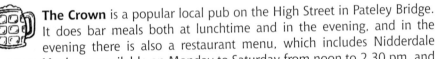

The Crown is a popular local pub on the High Street in Pateley Bridge. It does bar meals both at lunchtime and in the evening, and in the evening there is also a restaurant menu, which includes Nidderdale trout. Meals are available on Monday to Saturday from noon to 2.30 pm, and from 6.30 pm to 9 pm; and on Sunday from noon to 3 pm. The real ales are John Smith's and Theakstone. The Crown also does bed and breakfast, but there is no parking. Telephone: 01423 712455.

The Walk

Like every other Yorkshire dale, Nidderdale used to be full of industry: up on Greenhow there was extensive lead mining and smelting, and the lower part of the dale below Pateley Bridge had a major linen industry. Pateley Bridge is a pleasant small town with an attractive main street. I like small local museums, and Nidderdale Museum at Pateley Bridge is one of the best I know.

① From the car park go along the riverside path, keeping the river on the right.

On the left is the former railway line from Harrogate to Pateley Bridge. At one time there was a further line, which went to the reservoirs at the top of the valley. (Visit the museum to learn more about the railway.)

Continue along the attractive path for about a mile. Eventually it becomes a walled lane, with a lake on the right and a former mill leat on the left.

② Turn right when a metalled road at **Glasshouses** is reached. Cross the bridge over the Nidd, and then go up a lane on the left, signed as a public path to Heyshaw and Guisecliff. (Note the well-proportioned Glasshouses Mill through the trees on the left.) Turn right at a row of cottages; continue up the lane past more cottages, and then go up a path into **Parker Wood**. Turn right immediately after the stile; then go up the hillside, passing hollies and rocks and keeping fairly close to an old wire fence on the right. Bear left, then right, and go past **Guisecliff Tarn** on the right. The path levels out and briefly descends; it then continues as an attractive level woodland path, passing a large rock on the left. Eventually the path leaves the wood and climbs steeply up the hillside to a large mast.

③ Go over a ladder stile, and then turn right and go round the fence that encloses the mast. (There are good views to the escarpment of the **North Yorkshire Moors** and to the **Yorkshire Wolds** beyond **York**.) Now enjoy a mile of high quality walking along the fine gritstone edge of **Guisecliff**, with increasingly impressive views up **Nidderdale** beyond **Pateley Bridge**. The path retreats behind a wall towards the end, but there is a good view of **Greenhow Hill** nevertheless. Go over a ladder stile and down a rocky path to the road.

The strange gritstone building just after the stile is Yorke's Folly,
erected by John Yorke, a local landowner, to provide work during a time of unemployment around 1800. The men's wages included a loaf of bread each day.

④ Cross the road to a gate; go on a clear path for 30 yards, and then strike left across the moor on a vague path that soon peters out. The line you want is well to the left of a tree on the horizon, and there are low white posts to guide you. Cross the wall by a step stile and continue in the same direction on an indistinct path marked by further white posts. When the path peters

YORKE'S FOLLY AND GREENHOW HILL

out, gradually drop down to the stream, **Fosse Gill**, and ford it close to the top of a substantial waterfall. (If the water is dangerously high, go back to the road, and take the footpath into **Bewerley** and **Pateley Bridge**.)

Having crossed **Fosse Gill**, go upstream for a few yards, and then strike up the hillside for about 300 yards in a north-westerly direction, along a faint path if you can find it. Turn right when an unmetalled road is reached. Shortly after a gate, turn left along a clear path that goes across the moor and to the right of some evergreens, before dropping to a road.

⑤ Go straight across the road and down an access road to a house. Turn left briefly, then right, and go through a gap stile on the right-hand side of the house. Drop down a steep hillside through newly planted trees, and turn left along the unmetalled road at the bottom. Climb up to **Gillbeck Farm**; then take the 'preferred temporary permissive route' along an enclosed path – do not take the path to the left. Go through a gate; then cross the left-hand corner of the field to a step stile over the wall. There is no clear path after the stile, but keep in the same direction up the hillside, making first for a wooden pylon and then for a stile beside a gap in the wall straight ahead. Go well to the

left of the dilapidated wall in the next field and through a gap stile in the far corner. Then keep close to the wall on the left, and climb over a difficult stile beside a gate to the B6265 **Pateley Bridge–Grassington road**.

⑥ Cross the B6265 to a footpath sign; go through a narrow belt of trees, and then continue in the same direction, keeping close to a wall on the right. The path soon descends steeply, and there are good views of the upland valley straight ahead. Go to the left of the house at **Ivin Waite** and onto the access road, which goes quite steeply down the side of the valley. Turn right at the road junction and continue along a narrow metalled lane that soon leads into an open field. Keep going along the road for about half the length of the field; then slant left (there is no clear path) to the wall at the far side. Turn left and follow the track beside the wall as it drops down into the valley; this attractive route has good views and passes a fine Scots pine.

⑦ When the path reaches the bottom of the valley at **Mosscarr Bottom**, turn right immediately after a farm gate; go up a walled path and past a sweet chestnut tree, such trees are uncommon hereabouts. Stay close to the wall on the left when the path comes into a field, and in the next field slant right

THE PUB IN THE HIGH STREET AT PATELEY BRIDGE

on a clear path. After the gate, keep by the wall on the right to the far corner of the field, and then climb up a short field to a metalled road.

⑧ Turn left for a short distance, and when the road reaches a wood go down a footpath on the left, by a footpath sign. The path keeps close to the right-hand side of two large fields as it descends into **Pateley Bridge**. When a road is reached, briefly turn right, and then left down an alley which leads to the B6265. Cross the bridge over the **River Nidd**; then go a few yards up the **High Street** to the **Crown**, which is on the left.

 Date walk completed:

FELL BECK, BRIMHAM ROCKS AND EAVESTONE LAKE

BRIMHAM ROCKS

Distance:
12 miles

Starting Point:
The Half Moon Inn
at Fell Beck. GR
200662

Map: OS Explorer 298, Nidderdale

How to get there: *Fell Beck, also spelt Fellbeck, is a
scattered settlement 8 miles south-west of Ripon on the
B6265 to Pateley Bridge. The Half Moon Inn is on the
right of the B6265 at the bottom of a hill.*

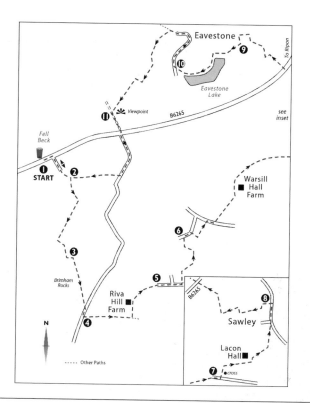

B etween Ripon and the lower end of Nidderdale is a landscape of pastures, woodland, and steep-sided valleys. Rock is never far below the surface, and gritstone crags crop up in all sorts of unexpected places, such as the famous and ever popular Brimham Rocks, owned by the National Trust. Most of the walk, though, is through lonely countryside where you are unlikely to meet many other walkers. It is a good walk for spotting wildlife – if you are lucky you will see deer, hares, and a wide variety of birdlife – and it has some excellent viewpoints.

Much of the land covered on this walk would have been owned in medieval times by nearby Fountains Abbey, a former Cistercian monastery, and many of the tracks would have led to it. The impressive remains of the monastery, a mile to the east of Sawley, are now a World Heritage site.

The Half Moon Inn at Fell Beck is a popular, friendly pub, which many years ago was a farmhouse. It offers a wide selection of main courses, including char grills, overseas dishes, and specials. Meals are available between noon and 2 pm and from 7 pm to 9 pm every day. The real ales are Black Sheep and Timothy Taylor's. Accommodation is available. Telephone: 01423 711560.

The Walk

① After leaving The Half Moon at Fell Beck, turn left up the **B6265** towards Ripon, and walk up the road for 200 yards as far as a postbox, where you turn right. Go along a side road which soon becomes a delightful walled green lane as it climbs the hillside.

Glance back to enjoy attractive countryside of woodland and stone-walled pasture, with moorland in the background.

② Turn sharp right when the lane leads into a field, and follow the line of telephone posts to **North Pasture**, where there is a stile beside the gate. Turn right in the farmyard, and then carry straight on through a stile at the end of the buildings. The path continues in more or less the same direction across fields (there are gates, not stiles) before merging with an unmetalled road. After a few yards, go over the stile on your left into the National Trust estate of **Brimham Rocks**. Follow the path, which keeps close to the wall on the left, and then gradually veers right through rocks, bilberry bushes, and heather to the woodland at the foot of the rocks. Turn right when you reach the bottom of the rocks, and then go left through a gap in the rocks to a wide, well-used track; this is the main access path through Brimham Rocks.

③ Turn right along the path, which soon goes past **Brimham House** on the left and then winds past spectacular crags of various shapes. You may well want to spend some time wandering amongst the rocks and the attractive oak and birch woodland. There is also a fine view from the trig point just at the back of Brimham House, and on a clear day you can see as far as the **Yorkshire Wolds** and the cooling towers of lower **Aire Valley**.

④ Follow the path past the car park to a metalled road. Turn right for a few yards, and then go left on a path marked 'public footpath Riva Hill'. The path goes across attractive moorland, though it gradually seems to be reverting to scrub. Shortly after the gate at the end of the moor, turn left along the lane to **Riva Hill Farm**. Keep straight on through a narrow gate at the side of a barn (watch the drop at the other side); then go down the field for a few yards and through a gate on the right. Slant across the field to a gate near the far left-hand corner, and then turn right on a woodland path that soon leads to a lane.

⑤ Turn left along the lane and keep straight on for about a third of a mile, ignoring the bridle path to the right and the metalled road to the left. Just before a house on the right,

go over a stile beside a gate on the left, and keep by the hedge as you go up the field. Go left of the gate straight ahead, but shortly afterwards go through a gate on the right. Cut diagonally across the field to a gate at the far side; keep by the wall on your right in the next field, and then slant across the following field to a gate leading to **South East Farm** and a metalled road.

⑥ Turn right along the road past a high crag. Shortly after, go through a gate on the right marked 'paddock, ball games and play area' (a notice intended for the adjacent caravan

THE HALF MOON INN AT FELL BECK

site), and turn left almost immediately, making for the corner of the nearby wood. (There are extensive views southwards across to the radar balls on Menwith Hill.) The path keeps the wood on the left before coming to a road. Turn right, and soon after turn left at the footpath sign and go through two fields to **Warsill Hall Farm**. Go through the gate on your left, immediately before the farm, and then over a stile in the wall on the right. Cross the field to a gate at the far corner, which can be muddy, and then veer right, close to the fence. Go through a gate (again, muddy) and across the next field to a gate into the wood. Descend rapidly through the trees to **Butterton Bridge**, which is scarcely noticeable. Turn left (note the lake straight ahead), and then almost immediately turn right. The track goes steeply up the hillside to a gate and then slants across a field to a gate in the far right corner.

⑦ Just after a conveniently placed seat, go over a stile on the left and cut diagonally across the field (**Lacon Cross** is just on the right). Go over the stile and down the field, making for the right-hand side of **Lacon Hall**. Be prepared to negotiate lots of mud before going over a stile into the garden; then turn sharp left at the end of the buildings, and go down the road and into a field. Veer left off the

access road to a well-concealed stile close to the corner of the field. Cross the next field to the hedge; then turn left, keeping the hedge on your right. Continue in the same direction across the next field to a stile. Carry straight on along the road past **Sawley church** and the Sawley Arms to reach the village green, where you turn left along the hedge.

⑧ Just before the swings and slides, go over the stile on the left; then keep the hedge close to your right as the path climbs two fields. The path then turns sharp right, crosses a stile, and then turns sharp left along a hedge. Turn right immediately after the stile. (There are good views at this point across to the Hambleton Hills and the Cleveland escarpment.) Then go through three fields to reach the **B6265** road. Turn left for a few yards, and then turn right along a farm road to **Gowbusk**. Turn left at the farmhouse through a waymarked but concealed gate. Turn right along another farm road and go straight on at the farm on the left. Bear left, immediately after the farm, keeping the hedge close on your left. Turn sharp left at the next stile, negotiate a very wet few yards, and then bear left to **Hollin Hill Farm**. Keep straight on along the lane for a short distance, and then go over a stile on the right.

⑨ Slant across the field to a stile leading into **Fishpond Wood**. The path descends steeply to **Eavestone Lake**. Go across the dam, and turn left along a wooded path by the lake. (This is a delightful scene of water, woodland, and crags, an ideal spot to rest for a few minutes.) Continue along the path, cross the bridge, from which there are good views of the crags by the upper lake, and climb up the hill to a metalled road.

⑩ Turn right and follow the road into the hamlet of **Eavestone**. Keep straight on past the cul-de-sac sign to a gate into a green lane. Shortly afterwards turn left, keeping the fence on your left as you descend into a shallow valley and climb the other side. Go through the gate, then through another gate on the right, and up the farm track towards **Brim House Farm**. Go over the stile and turn right; then immediately after the gate turn left along a track beside a wall. Keep dead straight through several fields, with Eavestone Moor nearby on the right, to the top of the hill.

This unnamed modest height is a fine viewpoint. Straight across Nidderdale to the south-west are the wooded crags of Guisecliff and beyond it Greenhow Hill, Lord's Seat, and Simon's Seat. Just to the left is the unmistakeable round lump of Round Hill, with Beamsley Beacon close by. In the opposite direction, you can see for miles across the Vale of York.

⑪ Turn left along the farm road and cross the **B6265**. Continue in the same direction for half a mile along a metalled road with good views across Nidderdale. Turn right along a farm road by the bridleway sign, and keep straight on through a gate and into a field with a wall close by on the right. Things should begin to look familiar when you reach the gate at the bottom of the field. Go down the walled lane that you toiled up earlier in the day and soon you are back on the B6265, close to **The Half Moon**.

Date walk completed:

MASHAM, ILTON AND THE RIVER URE

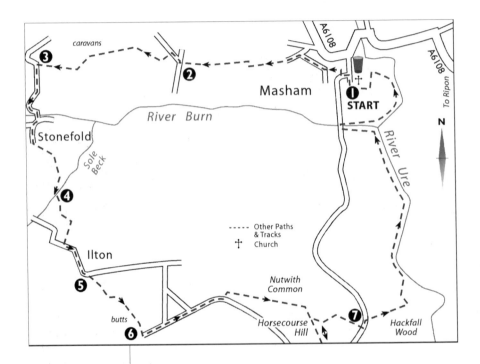

Distance:
12 miles

Starting Point:
The Bruce Arms,
Masham
GR 224808.
There is plenty of
parking space on
the adjacent main
market square.

Map: OS Explorer 298, Nidderdale; OS Explorer 302,
Northallerton and Thirsk

How to get there: Masham is 10 miles north-west of
Ripon. When coming into Masham on the A6108 from
Ripon, cross the bridge over the River Ure, and then take
the first turn left to the town centre and market place.

HAWTHORN BLOSSOM ON A LANE NEAR NUTWITH COMMON

*T*his walk explores a landscape of woodland and pasture between the valley of the River Ure and the Pennine moors. Our route goes into the lower end of Colsterdale, one of Yorkshire's least known dales, and then climbs up the valley of Sole Beck to the edge of the moors at Ilton. The return is through the extensive woodland of Nutwith Common, and then beside a scenic section of the River Ure. The walk touches the edge of Hackfall Woods, a large 18th-century landscape garden, which fell into disuse and became overgrown, but has now been restored by the Woodland Trust.

Most of the paths are sparsely trodden – even those on the Ripon Rowel, a splendid circular walk – but they provide enjoyable walking, with many fine views. Late April, when the leaves are just coming out and the hedgerows and banks are full of spring flowers, is a particularly good time to do this walk.

The **Bruce Arms** is on Little Market Place at the northern end of the main market square in Masham. It is a welcoming small pub, which provides lunches and evening meals, including steak and ale pie, roasts, and European dishes. There is also a Sunday lunch. Meals are available from 10 am to 8.30 pm Wednesdays to Sundays, and 10 am to 3 pm on Mondays and Tuesdays. The real ales are Black Sheep, John Smith's and Tetley. Accommodation is also available. Telephone: 01765 689372.

The Walk

Masham is a small North Yorkshire town, well known for its breweries. The large market square, with the spire of the church in the background, makes an attractive scene. Tall spires are not common in this part of Yorkshire, and Masham's is a much loved landmark for miles around.

① Leave the main square of Masham by **Church Street**, which is at the opposite end of the square to the church. Turn right after the HSBC bank, and then turn left on a walled path beside **Theakston's brewery**, an attractive limestone building. Turn right at the end and go along **Westholme Road**; then turn left across the roadbridge over the diminutive **Swinney Beck**. Immediately after Jameson's animal feeds factory, you are on a pleasant green lane that climbs gently into fields, with good views of the moors and hills in the distance. Keep to the left of a barn; then go through a gate on the right, and almost immediately a gate on the left. Follow a farm track through three fields, but leave the track in the next field and keep by the hedge on the right . The clear path now keeps close to the hedge until it comes to a metalled road.

② Go across and beside the road for a few yards, and then over a stile on the left by a footpath sign. (The next mile is on an enjoyable right of way with pleasant views of **Lower Colsterdale**. The path has only recently been rescued from a completely impassable state. It goes across lots of narrow fields that extend outwards from the nearby village of **Fearby**. Although it is waymarked, it is not easy to follow: hence the detailed directions.) Go along the hedge, and then over a stile on the right. Slant across the corner of the field to another stile; then continue in the same direction to a stile to the right of some tall hawthorns. Cross a narrow field to a wooden plank bridge and a stile; then go through the gate at the far right corner of the next field. The path now keeps along the hedge on the right – don't go over the stile, which is the path to **Fearby**. Go through three gates and then a stile, and in the next field slant across to the right to a stile in the corner. Keep along the hedge in the next field; then cross to the left corner of the field with the caravans, where there is a gate and missing stile. Keep by the hedge on the left in the caravan field; then go over a stile and across to a stile by a white tank. Veer left across the next field, which may have crops, to a stile near the far left corner;

then keep close to the hedge on the right until it peters out. Now cross the field towards a building (a primary school) on the skyline, and come to a metalled road by a footpath sign.

③ Turn left down the road, which is pleasant and only lightly used, and go over the bridge across the **River Burn**, the river that runs through **Colsterdale**. At the road junction, turn right; then soon after go left through a metal gate and up to the farm at **Stonefold**. Immediately after the farm, bear left to a stile; then go over another stile on the

THE WELCOMING BRUCE ARMS AT MASHAM

left. Cut across the corner of the field to a gate; then go left and through the gate at the bottom of a row of oaks. Go along the hedge on the left and then along a track to a gate. Continue along the track in the next field, past some fine oaks, and then drop to a stile some yards below the gate. Continue along the valley bottom; go over a stile and then on a footbridge across **Sole Beck**. This is another **Pennine** secret valley, and a delightful place.

④ Cross a stile by a post with waymarks; then go over a stile in the wall on the left. The next field is boggy in places and overgrown with bracken. The easiest thing is to go straight to the fence at the top; then turn right, and keep going along a track. Eventually, go through a stone gap stile by a sycamore. Climb the hillside to the right of a large sycamore, and then go well to the right of a small white building. Cross a stream by a stone slab, and climb the next field by the wall on the right. Pause at the top to enjoy the view; then turn right and keep along the fence. Go to the left of a stone barn; then bear left through a gate and go up the slope to a telephone box. This is **Ilton**. Now turn left along the metalled road to a road junction by a small triangle of grassland beside a stone shelter.

⑤ Go straight across by a Ripon Rowel footpath sign, then tread

gently across marshy ground to a stile at the corner of the walls. After a few yards, go over a stile on the left; then cross the field to a clump of oaks on the right and go up the hillside to a step stile onto the moor.

This is a fine viewpoint. Straight ahead is the impressive escarpment of the North Yorkshire Moors, and the triangular peak is Roseberry Topping, near Great Ayton. Further to the left is Middlesbrough.

Turn left along the wall; then go along the grouse butts on the right. Veer slightly right after the last butt; then turn left along the wall to a gate at the corner of the moor, which you go through onto a lane. (The direct route to the gate is not a right of way.)

⑥ Walk straight down the lane. (This is a quiet, pleasant lane, with many hawthorns and rowans, and good views which include the spire of **Masham church**.) Turn left into the woodland of **Nutwith Common** by the notice inscribed 'Swinton Estate Woodland', and then immediately take a broad unsurfaced track to the right through stately beeches. After nearly a mile, bear right at the junction with another track. In 200 yards or so, watch out for a yellow blob on a tree on the right, and veer right here along another unsurfaced track. Soon afterwards turn right at another yellow blob (plus arrow), and soon you come to a gate stile at the edge of the wood. Continue on the path up the slope – the side of **Horsecourse Hill** – and you get a surprise view stretching to **Roseberry Topping** and **Middlesbrough**. Retrace your steps, and go through the gate again; then turn right and keep along the wall. Soon you will come to a broad track that leads down to the road from **Masham** to **Grewelthorpe**.

⑦ Go left for a few yards; then turn right at the footpath sign by a splendid sycamore, and descend the hillside. Ignore the path signed to **Hackfall Wood**, and keep straight on by the hedge on the left. The path now enters **Hackfall Wood**, a delightful stretch of mixed woodland. Soon turn left through a gate into a field. (If you carry straight on you quickly come to a stretch of the River Ure where you can play in the sand.) Keep close to the fence on the right for a short distance; then go through a gate. The path descends through dark woodland to the **River Ure**, and

then continues along the bank before coming out into a field. Keep fairly close to the river bank in the next three fields. (The dilapidated building on the left was a dovecote.) Then continue along the side of the river on a fenced path that requires care in places. (The latter part of the path is actually alongside the **River Burn**.) Turn right at the road and cross the bridge; then immediately take a path on the right, which soon comes back to the Ure. Continue along the riverside path (good for spring flowers), and after the water treatment works keep along the access road by the hedge on the left. Go over a wooden step stile on the left and up a short hillside to a kissing gate; then turn right into the attractive churchyard.

Masham church has a Norman tower beneath its spire, and there is the base of a Saxon cross near the south porch.

After looking round the church, cross the market square to the **Bruce Arms**.

Date walk completed:

WEST BURTON AND WENSLEYDALE SCARS

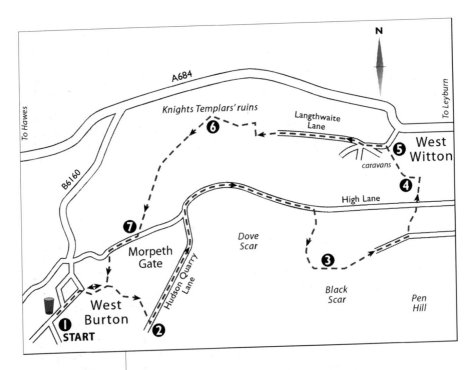

Distance:
9 miles

Starting Point:
The Fox and
Hounds, West
Burton.
GR 017867

Map: OS Outdoor Leisure 30, Yorkshire Dales, Northern and Central Areas

How to get there: *Go from Leyburn along the A684 towards Hawes. After 6 miles, turn left along the B6160; West Burton is reached after 1¾ miles. Turn left into the main part of the village, and the Fox and Hounds is on the right-hand side of the green.*

HUDSON QUARRY LANE

*N*early all circular walks are better done one way round rather than the other, but with this walk the decision was a particularly difficult one. If I feel my ears burning, it may well be because heavily sweating walkers are cursing me vehemently – if they have any breath left – as they labour up the steep hill at the start of the walk. However, it gets a lot of the climbing over and done with, and you can pause for wonderful views at more or less every step. Furthermore, there is the consoling prospect that the last few miles are very easy going. This is a good choice for a winter walk, as it is fairly dry underfoot.

The route includes several *scars* – rocky edges that make the hillsides rise in a series of gigantic steps. They are very hard strands of rock that have been more resistant to weathering and the movements of ice. Their sides are often wooded, sycamore being the dominant species, and along the top of them there is excellent, fairly level walking often on walled green lanes; Hudson Quarry Lane and Langthwaite Lane are a particular delight. Most of the scars are limestone, but the appropriately named Black Scar is hard gritstone. Scars are not exclusive to Wensleydale, but it is a good area for appreciating them.

The Fox and Hounds is a delightful small village pub, and dates back to the 18th century. It offers a wide range of main courses and specials, including fisherman's platter, pub curry, steak and kidney pie, and venison casserole, as well as grills and pizzas. Meals are available every day from noon to 2.30 pm (3 pm on Sundays), and from 6.30 pm to 9 pm. Real ales are Black Sheep, Hambleton, Skipton, and Tetley. Accommodation is also available. Telephone: 01969 663111.

The Walk

West Burton is at the bottom of Bishopdale, surrounded by high hills and moors. It is an idyllic Yorkshire Dales village, with stone-built houses lining each side of the attractive village green. It has never had a parish church, but it still has a school, a pub, and a butcher's; so village institutions are surviving quite well.

① Walk past the butcher's shop and 'Moorside Cats' to the bottom right-hand corner of the village green. Turn sharp right by a footpath sign, with a large sycamore tree straight ahead. The scene changes dramatically as a wide rocky stream, **Walden Beck**, is reached, and there is a high waterfall about 100 yards further up. Go over the footbridge and take the path up the steps by the wall. Turn right by the gate, and go up the hillside just to the right of a stone barn. Then continue in the same direction to a stile into the wood. Turn right on the path signed

'Hudson Quarry Lane'. The attractive path climbs steeply up the side of the wood, through a gap stile, and under an immense ash tree. It goes through hawthorns to a step stile, and then zigzags up the steep hillside. (There is a marvellous view of **West Burton**, **Bishopdale**, and the **Walden Valley**.) After a stile and then a post, climb up the field towards a farm gate in front of a limestone scar, the continuation of **Dove Scar**.

② At the top of the field, turn left along **Hudson Quarry Lane**, signed to **Morpeth Gate**. It soon becomes an attractive grassy, walled lane as it gradually descends to **Morpeth Scar**. (There are fine views to the left over **Wensleydale**.) When **Morpeth Gate** comes up from the left, carry straight on beneath a canopy of larch and sycamore trees. The lane, now called **High Lane**, is stony in places but there is plenty of short grass to walk on for much of the time. You might also find orchids in the spring. (**Pen Hill** comes into view on the right and the **Cleveland Hills** can be seen in the distance.) After about a mile, go through a gate on the right by a footpath sign for **Black Scar**. The path goes up a field to a gate near the top right-hand corner and climbs steeply up the next field, keeping close to the wall. (This climb has been up the eastern continuation of **Dove Scar**. The bleak northern face of **Pen Hill** is straight ahead.) Go through a gate at the top of the field, and continue along a clear path on level ground. When the path divides, take the right-hand option and continue to a metal trough by a tumbledown wall. (If you want to climb **Black Scar**,

strike off right to some old quarries; then go up a path that keeps close to a deep V-shaped cleft in the hillside. Regrettably, there is no right of way along Black Scar to Pen Hill.)

③ Continue along the path after the metal trough; then veer left to a stile beside a gate at the far left corner of the field. Continue along the track by the wall on the right.

There are good views ahead of the magnificent escarpment (surely the best in England!) that forms the western edge of the North Yorkshire Moors, and runs

THE FOX AND HOUNDS ON THE VILLAGE GREEN AT WEST BURTON

more or less unbroken from Sutton Bank near Thirsk to Kildale.

The track soon leads into a walled lane called **Flint Lane**. After about a half mile, go through a gap stile on the left – if it is a gated stile, you've gone too far. Rapidly descend the steep hillside, crossing two scars on the way. (Note the Middleham racecourse gallops beyond the farm on the right.) In the second field the path veers slightly right to cross a lane and then continues in the same direction to a stile. Keep close to a wall on the left in the next field; then turn left after a gate stile.

④ Immediately after a stone barn on the right, the path slants right and crosses a belt of newly planted trees. It then goes through a gate stile and over a footbridge into a caravan site. Keep left of the access road and go along an enclosed footpath between the caravans. Cross the access road to a path by a cypress hedge, and descend through a wood to a metalled road.

⑤ Turn left along the road, and shortly afterwards turn right along **Langthwaite Lane**, a walled lane, signed as a public footpath to **Templars Chapel**. Langthwaite Lane is a delightful green lane with good views, especially over to **Bolton Castle** on the right and to **Pen Hill** on the left. When the lane ends, go over the stile into the field and continue in the same direction to a gate at the left-hand corner. Cross the next field to a stile by the right-hand gate, and then slant down the hillside. Turn right down the unfenced lane, and after a short distance turn left and keep close to a wall on the right beside a wood. Go through a gate and slant across the next field to the right-hand corner.

Just before the corner is a fenced-off area enclosing the remnants of a chapel built by the Knights Templar around 1200. Visitors are unlikely to gape in awe at the few remaining stones and graves of the chapel, but it is a pleasant spot to linger for a few minutes.

⑥ Now take the footpath signed to **Morpeth Gate**, and walk along a delightful meadowland path, with fine views towards **Bishopdale**. After about a mile the path goes through a gate near some ash trees, and at the end of the next field it comes to **Morpeth Gate**.

⑦ Turn right and go down the unsurfaced lane for about a third of a mile to a stile on the left signed '**West Burton by Barrack Wood**'. The stile is immediately after a holly bush on the left and is easy to miss. (If you fail to find it and carry straight on, the lane will soon come into **West Burton**, but it would be a shame to do it this way, as a fine

A LIMESTONE SCAR AND THE WALDEN VALLEY

ending to the walk will be missed.) Go along an attractive path into **Barrack Wood** and through a gate stile on the right by a footpath sign. (Don't go straight on, or you will be doing the walk again!) Retrace your steps of earlier in the day, first down to the bridge over **Walden Beck**, and then up the village green to the pub.

Date walk completed:

BAINBRIDGE, SEMER WATER, CRAGDALE AND ADDLEBROUGH

THE ROSE AND CROWN AT BAINBRIDGE

Distance:
14 miles

Starting Point:
The Rose and
Crown at
Bainbridge.
GR 934903

Map: OS Outdoor Leisure 30, Yorkshire Dales, Northern and
Central Areas

How to get there: Bainbridge is 10 miles west of
Leyburn on the A684. It can be reached easily from the
A1, by turning onto the A684 at Leeming Bar. The Rose
and Crown is at the far end of the village green in
Bainbridge.

*T*he start of the walk is along the brief but beautiful valley of the River Bain. The route then goes beside Semer Water, one of Yorkshire's rare natural sheets of water, and on into the little-known valley of Cragdale. From there it climbs the hills separating Wensleydale from upper Wharfedale, and then drops down to Carpley Green before crossing the summit of Addlebrough, the craggy limestone hill that dominates the middle part of Wensleydale. The final stretch traverses one of Wensleydale's wooded scars before returning to Bainbridge.

At nearly 14 miles, the walk is rather long but I regard it as the best circuit for including Addlebrough, and every step is a delight. If, towards the end of the walk, the ascent of the hill seems too much, you can take three miles off by going straight down the lane from Carpley Green to Bainbridge. However, it is an option to be avoided if at all possible, as Addlebrough is one of the most enjoyable hills in the Pennines, with fine views of Wensleydale from the top and all the way down.

This is a beautiful walk at any time, but to fully appreciate it I think I would opt for late May or June, when the meadows are full of flowers, the sweet-smelling wild thyme is coming out on the limestone uplands, and you will still be able to hear the cry of the curlew and lapwing as well as the churr of the wheatear.

The Rose and Crown Hotel at the far end of Bainbridge village green is an old coaching inn dating back to the 15th century. It has a wide range of main courses in the bar, including steaks, Thai green chicken curry, and wild mushroom risotto, and there is also a restaurant menu. Meals are available from 12 noon to 2.15 pm, and from 6 pm to 9.30 pm. The real ales are Black Sheep, Webster's, and Theakston's Old Peculier. The hotel is residential, and has 11 rooms. Telephone: 01969 650225.

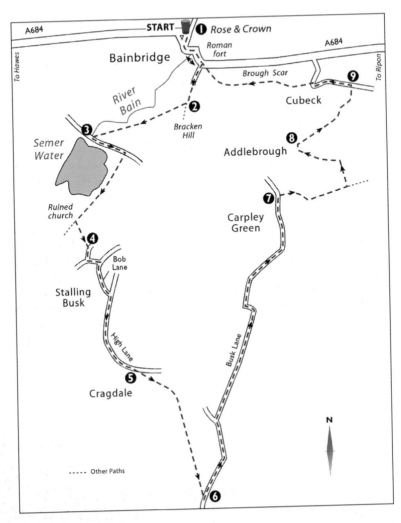

The Walk

Bainbridge is an attractive Wensleydale village built around a large village green. It was a quite important place in Roman times when there was a fort, Virosidum, on the small rounded hill to the east of the village. At the edge of the village green, by the River Bain, is Low Mill, a restored cornmill, which can be visited by appointment.

① Leave **Bainbridge** in a south-easterly direction by the A684 across the village green. Continue on the main road across the bridge over the **River Bain** (casting a glance at the waterfalls on the right), and go up the hill for 100 yards or so. Just before the road junction, take the path on the right signed to **Semer Water**. The well-marked path climbs gently beside the valley of the **Bain**.

② Take the right-hand one of two adjacent stiles in a wall near the top of **Bracken Hill**. There is no bracken and it isn't much of a hill, but it is a good viewpoint; so pause and enjoy the prospect. (There is a delightful scene of meadows, woodland, field barns, and nearby hills. **Semer Water** is now in view straight ahead, and the prominent limestone peak to its right is unnamed, surprisingly, and just marked 'crag' on the map.) Continue in more or less the same direction to the right of two trees in the foreground as the path descends through fields to the **River Bain**. (Here there is plenty of bird life, including herons and redshanks.) Walk beside the river to the splendid arch of **Semer Water Bridge**.

③ Turn left at the bridge. (The sweet-smelling plant by the stile is sweet cicely.) Walk along the lane beside **Semer Water**, with good views across the lake. Just after the lane leaves the lake, go over a vertiginous ladder stile on the right, and walk along an attractive path which is never far from the lakeside.

ADDLEBROUGH FROM ABOVE CARPLEY GREEN

The path climbs gently beyond the lake end and goes through a nature reserve. (Turn your head back occasionally for views of Semer Water.) Spare a few minutes to explore the ruins of a church dating from the 1600s; until c1900 it was the church for Stalling Busk, and has now been replaced by the small Swiss-style church in the village. Immediately after the ruined church, go through a gate, and take the path signed to **Stalling Busk**.

④ Turn right along the metalled road in Stalling Busk, passing the phone box and the postbox. At the T-junction, turn left up **Butts Lane**, and then, fairly soon, turn sharp right up **Bob Lane**, which climbs quite steeply up the side of the valley. Keep right when Bob Lane comes to **High Lane**, and enjoy the fine views to the right.

Three valleys come down from the hills to join Raydale at the upper end of Semer Water. The nearest one, still partly hidden, is Cragdale, beautiful, though sparsely endowed with crags.

⑤ After about half a mile, and just after a wood on the left, go through a stile on the right.

The noticeboard mentions 'a possible prehistoric field system' and also 'a very good chance of seeing buzzards'. I saw a buzzard

on a recent visit and it is a fine sight; buzzards are common in the West Country but they haven't really colonized the Pennines.

The splendid grassy path slants across the field to the left. After crossing a stream, carry on in the same direction up a hillside to a stile in the wall. The path then soon veers right to a stile in the far corner of the field, and then continues to a step stile across the next wall. Keep in the same direction in the next field, where the stile is easy to miss – don't drift right along the wall! – and then through two more fields until you reach a grassy lane. (This is the southernmost point of the walk.)

⑥ Turn sharp left along the lane, and, after half a mile, turn right along another grassy lane, **Busk Lane**. This is fine limestone upland country. When the lane begins to drop, the flat top of **Addlebrough** suddenly comes into view straight in front of you.

⑦ Just after the last barn of the farmstead at **Carpley Green**, turn right along the bridleway signed 'Thornton Rust'. Keep close to the wall on your right in the first field, and then go through fields beside a wide limestone valley on the right. When you reach the signpost in the fifth field, turn left on the permissive path. This climbs fairly gently at first, but when it gets to a post it swings left and climbs **Addlebrough** in earnest. The path becomes less distinct, but keeps in the same direction to a post at the top of the steepest part and then goes over a ladder stile on to the tabletop summit. If the weather is reasonably kind, it is well worth lingering for a while to enjoy the marvellous views over **Wensleydale**.

⑧ Leave **Addlebrough** to the north-east, by a white-topped post, and drop down steeply to a ladder stile at the right-hand corner of the field. The path descends through fields and over further vertiginous stiles. Though waymarked, it is not particularly easy to follow, but as a general rule keep fairly close to the shallow gully on the right, and, as you near the bottom, keep well to the right of the farm. Turn left when the metalled lane is reached.

⑨ When the lane turns sharp right at **Cubeck**, keep straight on through the farmstead, ignoring the lane to the left. The route through the farm buildings is waymarked, but not too easy to find. Take the right-hand one of the two gates at the end of the farm buildings, and veer across the field to a pylon. Turn slightly left here, and then go to the right of further farm buildings. In the next field, make for a gate beside a small ash tree, and then continue in the same direction to a gate at the far side of the following field. At the signpost just inside the next field, veer right to a gap stile into the wood. Now follow the delightful path along the top of **Brough Scar**. As you descend into **Bainbridge** at the end of the scar, there are good views of the Roman fort on the low hill to the right.

Date walk completed:

UPPER SWALEDALE FROM MUKER

FIELD BARNS NEAR THWAITE

Distance:
12 miles

Starting Point:
The Farmers'
Arms at Muker.
GR 910979

Map: OS Outdoor Leisure 30, Yorkshire Dales Northern and
Central Areas

How to get there: Muker is at the far end of Swaledale,
19 miles from Richmond. From Richmond, take the A6108
to Leyburn, and after 5 miles turn right along the B6270
and keep going up the valley.

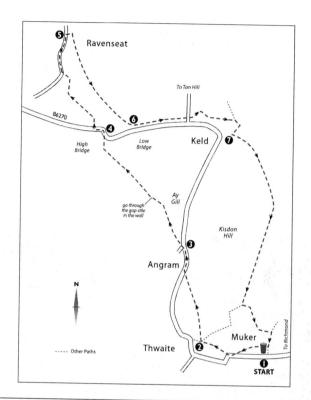

The special features of this walk are the limestone gorges; the many original hay meadows (i.e. not 'improved' by modern agro-chemicals), which are full of flowers in the early summer; and the many stone barns that give such a distinctive character to the countryside in Upper Swaledale. They were built in the 18th and 19th centuries and used to store hay and as shelter for cattle.

The upper end of Swaledale around Keld and Kisdon is for me quite simply one of the most beautiful places on earth, with its marvellous landscape of limestone crags, waterfalls, meadows, and woodland, backed by the darker peat moors. I once walked there on a sparkling November day when the leaves were still on the trees in their various autumnal hues, and the low sun gave the limestone a warm yellow glow, the whole scene enhanced by the deep red of the decaying bracken.

The Farmers' Arms is a welcoming small pub on the main road in the middle of Muker. Meals are available from 12 noon to 2.30 pm and from 6.30 pm to 8.45 pm. I recommend the home-made steak pie. Real ales are Black Sheep and Theakstone. A studio flat is available for weekly letting. Telephone: 01748 886297.

The Walk

Muker is a village beside the River Swale. The church with its squat tower is an attractive feature, though of no great age. Close to the pub and church is the literary institute, a charming small building with a Flemish-style façade. It was built in 1867 and used to house 600 books; it has provided a venue for concerts, lectures and meetings.

① Turn left out of the Farmers' Arms, and immediately turn left up the path at the side of the pub. Turn left at the top of the path, and go through a stile by a gate. Now follow the path across several fields, and then down to the farm buildings at **Usha Gap**. Turn right along the main road for a few yards, and then go through the stile on the right, immediately before the bridge. Now follow a clear path across meadows towards the village of **Thwaite**.

② Immediately before coming into **Thwaite**, take the second footpath on the right, signed to **Angram**. This goes to the right of a modern barn, and then turns left through a stile by a gate. The clear path then goes up the valley, past stone barns. **Kisdon Hill** rises steeply on the right; amongst the vegetation on its side is juniper, and patches of this attractive shrub are not uncommon in Swaledale.

After about a mile, the path climbs steeply up a meadow to the right of a barn before coming out on the main road again; turn right and follow the road into the small village of **Angram**.

③ Turn left at the phone box at the top of the village, and go through the gate on the right by the footpath sign. Climb up the steep hillside by an old wall, passing a limekiln on the left. The path continues in the same direction, climbing steadily across upland meadows. (There are fine views behind down the valley and across to **Kisdon Hill**.) The path goes into the shallow valley at the top end of **Ay Gill** and through a gap stile in the wall on the right. (**Take note**: do not carry straight on to a stile over the fence!) Turn left along the wall, and continue in the same direction across moorland on a fine airy path, which is clear to follow. Where the path fords a stream near a grouse butt, keep in the same direction up the other side of the shallow valley and cross the grouse-shooting track at a small cairn. The path soon becomes distinct again, goes over a ladder stile to the right of a barn, and eventually drops down to meet the **Kirkby Stephen–Keld road** at **High Bridge**, a sturdy stone bridge over **Birkdale Beck**.

(If you want to shorten the walk, turn right along the road to **Keld** at **High Bridge**, then go over the first bridge on the left, which is **Low Bridge**, to rejoin the main walk at 6.)

④ Cross the bridge, pausing to look over the side; go along the road for a few yards and then over the stile on the right. Climb up the field to a stile by the sycamore in the top right corner. Keep close to the wall on the right in the next two fields. When the wall finishes, keep going towards a barn straight ahead; then veer slightly right and go just to the left of the next two barns. (There are good views over to the deep gorge on the right.) After a ladder stile, keep going in the same direction

THE VILLAGE PUB IN MUKER

UPPER SWALEDALE, NEAR KELD

along the metalled road to the hamlet of **Ravenseat**, one of the most remote settlements in England.

⑤ Go over a narrow stone bridge as you come into **Ravenseat**; then turn right and go over another bridge. Just before the house straight ahead, turn right along the footpath signed to **Keld**. The path, which is part of the Coast to Coast Walk, goes down the valley and keeps close to the edge of the spectacular gorge on the right. There is more than one path when you come into the much larger field – actually part of the open moor – but make for the farm buildings at **Smithy Holme**, and then continue

along the farm track into the valley. ⑥ Just before the track crosses the river at **Low Bridge**, turn left at a waymarked post and go along an attractive path at the top of a wooded limestone scar, where there are lots of wild flowers and plenty of bird life. Cross the metalled road to **Tan Hill**, and continue along a farm track, with good views over to Keld on the right. Turn right at the farm buildings at **East Stonesdale** – you are now on the **Pennine Way** – and go down into the valley. This is a delightful spot with steep wooded hillsides and waterfalls, as well as convenient seats. Turn right immediately before the waterfall and continue on the **Pennine Way** into the bottom of the valley. Cross the bridge over the **Swale** and tackle the steep short climb at the other side.

A couple of centuries ago, Swaledale was an important lead-mining area, and Beldi Hill, at the other side of the river from Keld, now so beautiful, was once a hive of noxious industry. Over the hill, Gunnerside Valley would have been full of fumes from the smelting mills. Work in the lead industry must have been pretty vile: cold, wet, and poisonous. There were also many small coal pits on the moors in Swaledale, and the Tan Hill colliery, on the road from Keld to Tan Hill, produced coal well into the 20th century.

⑦ Turn sharp left at the top (if you want to see the small village of Keld,

turn right), and walk along an enjoyable wooded path with good views of the nearby gorge and limestone cliffs. Keep to the **Pennine Way** and ignore the path signed to **Muker**, which goes along the bottom of the valley and is a greatly inferior route. The **Pennine Way** now provides 2 miles of high quality walking along the steep eastern side of **Kisdon Hill**, with stunning views down into the valley below and across to **Swinner Gill**. The path eventually descends to a former cottage, where you leave the **Pennine Way** and turn left down a green lane which eventually becomes an unfenced farm road. (There are fine views down **Swaledale** as the track steeply descends the hillside towards **Muker**.) Avoid a left turn back up the valley, and continue along the lane to the village and the **Farmers' Arms**,

Date walk completed:

SETTLE, GIGGLESWICK SCAR, VICTORIA CAVE AND ATTERMIRE SCAR

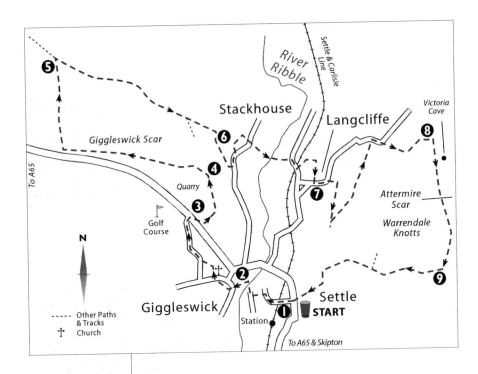

Distance:
10 miles

Starting Point:
The Golden Lion,
Duke Street, Settle.
GR 819635

Map: OS Outdoor Leisure 41, Forest of Bowland and Ribblesdale.

How to get there: *Settle is 16 miles from Skipton on the A65 road from Skipton to Kendal. Turn right onto the B6480 at the roundabout at the beginning of the Settle bypass, and keep straight on into Settle. The Golden Lion is in the middle of the town, on the right just before the market place but parking is limited. There is ample parking elsewhere in Settle, and there is also a good rail service.*

WARRENDALE KNOTTS, NEAR ATTERMIRE SCAR

*T*his walk is almost entirely on limestone. It goes first to the north-west of Settle, onto Giggleswick Scar, an attractive wooded limestone cliff, and then swings round to cross the Ribble Valley, traversing the magnificent countryside immediately to the east of Settle. With its dramatically shaped heights, steep crags, caves, and deep valley, it is as impressive as any limestone landscape in England. There are frequent views of Ingleborough and Penyghent, and all the Three Peaks can be viewed at once at one point on the walk. The attractive villages of Giggleswick and Langcliffe are visited on the way. This is a good walk to do at any time, but bear it in mind for a bright winter's day, when the low sun bathes the limestone with a warm glow and creates long dark contrasting shadows.

The Golden Lion is on Duke Street, and close to the town hall and market place. It was built around 1640, and still retains much of the atmosphere of a coaching inn. There is an extensive menu of individually prepared traditional and continental dishes, and a wide range of main course specials is available both at midday and in the evening. At lunchtime there is a good choice of lighter meals and in the evening an à la carte dinner menu. Meals are available Mondays to Fridays from 12 noon to 2.30 pm and from 6 pm to 9 pm (10 pm in the summer), on Saturdays from 12 noon to 10 pm, and on Sundays from 12 noon to 9 pm. The real ales are Thwaites. The hotel is residential and has 12 bedrooms. Telephone: 01729 822203.

The Walk

Settle is a small Pennine town of considerable charm, with a busy market whose charter was granted in 1249, and many attractive 17th and 18th-century houses. Settle is probably best known for the Settle and Carlisle Railway, which opened in 1875 and was built by the Midland Railway in order to avoid going over the tracks of a rival company via Ingleton and Tebay. A journey along the line, which takes a magnificent route across the head of Ribblesdale, Dentdale, Garsdale, and Wensleydale, is strongly recommended.

① Go down **Kirkgate**, which is opposite the town hall clock. (Straight ahead on the skyline is a large dome with an extended nipple; this is the chapel of Giggleswick School.) Go under the railway bridge and past Booths Supermarket. Turn left on the path that goes between Peter's Funeral Services and the fire station. Turn right when it comes to a road, and go round the corner of Kings Mill (now apartments). Go over the footbridge across the **River Ribble**. You are now in **Giggleswick**.

② Veer left up the hillside and go along a path between high walls. Turn right and go along **Bankwell Street** as far as **Giggleswick church**, a pleasant limestone edifice, dedicated to the obscure St Alkelda. Much of the building is 15th-century. Go through the lychgate and across the churchyard, and turn right briefly along a lane beside the church wall. Turn sharp left round the last of the houses; pass through two stone stiles and cross the manicured playing fields of **Giggleswick School**. Turn right when the metalled road is reached and continue along it to the T-junction with the former A65.

③ Cross the road to the low stile immediately to the right of the **Giggleswick Quarry** sign. The path climbs steeply up the hillside by the edge of the quarry. (I find it interesting to have such a close-up view of a modern quarry, though it will not be everyone's predilection.) At the top of the climb, there is an excellent view of **Penyghent**. Continue along the fence at the top of the quarry.

④ A few yards beyond the quarry, veer left to a post by a small cairn; then continue in the same direction along a clear path, past a footpath

sign and another cairn. You are now on **Giggleswick Scar**, which is a place of considerable significance to geologists, as it marks the edge of the great **Craven Fault.** Keep going along the attractive grassy path as it wends its way through the clint. (There are several caves on the right, most of them not immediately visible.) The path eventually swings right and goes across a succession of pastures, with **Ingleborough** rearing up magnificently straight ahead.

⑤ When you reach a shallow valley (about 1^1/$_2$ miles from the end of the quarry), go over a ladder stile by

DUKE STREET, SETTLE

an old stone sheepfold; then after a few yards turn sharp right and slant up the hillside. Tracks zigzag all over the place, but the line you want is just left of the tree on the horizon. Go over a ladder stile by a gate and then continue across two fields on an easy grassy track. Shortly after entering the third field by a gate – if it is difficult to open, try putting your foot under it! – go through a gate on the right, and then keep close to the wall on the left. When the wall turns left, keep straight on. (The impressive limestone hills straight ahead across the valley are **Warrendale Knotts**.) Go through the right-hand one of two gaps in the wall when the path descends to a shallow valley. Steer across the next field towards two ladder stiles, and go over the left-hand one. Continue in the same direction and drop steeply to a signpost.

⑥ Take the right-hand path, and keep the wall on your left. Go over a well-concealed stile, and turn left along the metalled road. Then turn left along a lane, right when the houses of **Stackhouse** are reached, and then right again. Go straight across the road and along a walled path signed 'FP Locks'. Cross the footbridge over the **Ribble**, a fine sight it is as it tumbles over the weir, and go up the lane straight ahead. Turn right at the top and go onto the B6479; cross the bridge over the Settle and Carlisle line, and then immediately turn left along an unsurfaced lane. Shortly afterwards go through a stile by a yellow post on the right, and on a clear path up the hillside. Turn right at the top and go along a walled lane which leads into the village of **Langcliffe**.

⑦ In **Langcliffe**, turn left on the road past the attractive village green – don't miss the noticeboard with the by-laws – and the primary school. Just before the speed de-restriction signs, go through the gate immediately on the right and up the steep path. Keep close to the wall as the path bends to the right, and continue to a gate stile and then to a ladder stile. Turn sharp left after the ladder stile onto a path by the wall. In the next field veer right as the path gently climbs towards the left-hand side of a belt of trees, enjoying the outstanding views of **Ingleborough, Penyghent,** and **Whernside** (just to the right of **Ingleborough**): the Three Peaks all at once! When the path comes back to the road, turn right on a narrow unfenced lane which climbs steadily by a wall on the right.

⑧ Shortly after a stone barn, turn right along a path signed to **Victoria Cave**. The path keeps close to **Attermire Scar**, and soon passes a notice warning of the dangers of visiting the cave, which is up on the left.

Victoria Cave has been rich in archaeological finds; the bones of many ancient animals have been found there, including elephants and hippopotami, as well as evidence of human use since 9000 BC. There are many other caves nearby.

When the path begins to drop steeply, go over a ladder stile on the right and descend into the bottom of the valley. The scenery is magnificent, particularly **Warrendale Knotts** on the right.

⑨ Turn right, keeping the wall on the left, and climb gently up the hillside. (Keep looking back to enjoy the whole scene.) Where the path divides near the entrance to a cave, take the right-hand route; this passes a stile from which **Warrendale Knotts** can be climbed. After a level section, the path drops rapidly into **Ribblesdale** and it is a dramatic finish to the walk. (Ingleborough is again prominent but Giggleswick Quarry appears as a nasty gash.) The path swings left and by a derelict barn enters a walled lane, which soon leads into **Settle**, where you descend into the market place by a choice of attractive streets.

Date walk completed:

Walk 20

INGLETON, CLAPHAM AND INGLEBOROUGH

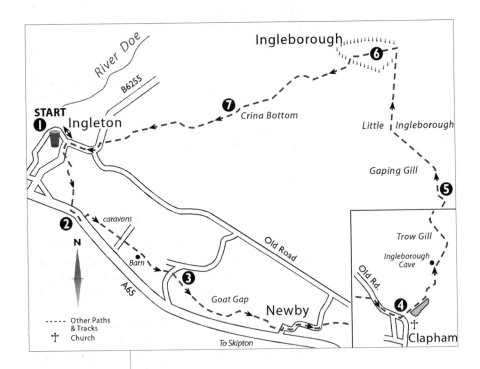

Distance:
12 miles

Starting Point:
The Wheatsheaf
Inn, Ingleton.
GR 696732

Map: OS Outdoor Leisure 2, Yorkshire Dales Southern &
Western Areas.

How to get there: *Ingleton is 27 miles from Skipton, on
the A65 road from Skipton to Kendall. Take the first turn
right after coming into Ingleton from Skipton, and then
turn right onto Main Street, which leads to High Street and
the Wheatsheaf.*

INGLEBOROUGH, SEEN FROM CRINA BOTTOM

*N*o book of adventurous walks in West Yorkshire and the Dales would be complete without Ingleborough. At 2,184 ft above sea level, it isn't the highest hill in Yorkshire – that distinction belongs to its near neighbour, Whernside – but it is simply the best: a brilliant viewing point and a splendid climb.

The excursion starts with a pleasant meadow walk from Ingleton to Clapham, the starting point of what is in my opinion the best way up Ingleborough. The route to the top is full of variety and interest and passes by Ingleborough Cave and Gaping Gill. The best way down from the summit is the direct route to Ingleton by Crina Bottom; for almost the whole of the descent there are views of Morecambe Bay – I love seeing the sea from hills – it is sheer delight!

The Wheatsheaf traces its history back to the 17th century and is a former coaching inn. One of the upstairs rooms was used as a courthouse, where JPs met to renew licences and deal with petty crime. The pub has an extensive blackboard menu of home-cooked main courses. Meals are available every day from noon to 2.30 pm, and from 6 pm to 9 pm. The real ales are Black Sheep, Taylors Landlord, and Tetley. The Wheatsheaf is residential and has nine bedrooms. Telephone: 01524 241275.

 # The Walk

Make sure you do this walk in bright weather; not to do so would be to miss the views and that would take away much of the enjoyment. Lastly, a warning: don't leave yourself short of time. Ingleborough is not a good place to get benighted. The timing of the walk is roughly two hours to Clapham, another two hours to the top of Ingleborough, and just over an hour down into Ingleton. That means starting not later than mid-morning in the winter months.

① Turn right from **the Wheatsheaf** and go up the **High Street**; then turn right shortly afterwards by a sign for the village centre and a stone post inscribed 'La Chapelle des Marais 500 miles'. After a short distance, turn left at the footpath sign by **Bower Cottage**. Go through the gate at the end of the cottages; then continue in the same direction across two small fields. Continue in the same direction in the third field, and then go through a stile on the right to a cul-de-sac between houses. Go along the road for about 100 yards, and then over a stile on the left, immediately after the last house. Keep along the side of the houses; then veer slightly right to a stile, and then a footbridge near the far corner of the field. (There are excellent views of **Ingleborough**.) Continue in the same direction to another stile, and then go across a field to the A65.

Just to the left over the last few fields is the former railway line from Clapham Junction – not the one in London! – to Tebay and Carlisle. A wrangle about running rights amongst the railway companies led to the building of the Settle to Carlisle line.

② Go along the A65 for a few yards, and then turn left into **Greenwood Leghe Holiday Home Park**. The right of way goes along the metalled access road through a beautiful avenue of trees. When the holiday homes are reached, you will be confronted by a sign with a rather ambiguous instruction; what you must do is turn right immediately after a wall juts out on the right. The path then goes round the side of the site with the holiday homes on your left. When the path comes to a lane, keep straight on to a T-Junction. (If you look back, you will see the **Lake District fells**.) Go over the stile opposite the end of the lane, and then make for the stone barn straight ahead. Go over a ladder stile and a footbridge, and then through a gate just to the left of the barn. Continue in the same direction with a wall on the left;

then, after a stile by a gate, veer left to the footpath signs to the left of another barn.

③ Cross the metalled road, and go over a stone step stile. The line of the path is between the two trees where there is a footbridge and across the field to a ladder stile near the far right corner. There is a stile near the right-hand corner of the next field, and then the path keeps close to the fence on the right, through fields to farm buildings at **Goat Gap**. Go over the stile by the gate and then down a passage with the farmhouse immediately on the

THE WHEATSHEAF, AT INGLETON

right. Cross a stream by a delightful stone bridge, and then veer left across the field and go through a farm gate. Turn right by the wall, and then cross a step stile. (The bumpy landscape beyond **Settle** has now come into view straight ahead. If you look back, you can still see the **Lake District fells**.) Keep close to the wall on the right; then cross it by a step stile, and keep close to it on the left. The path goes through a gate, over two stiles, and then to the right of an ash tree to another stone step stile. Keep the wall on your right and then go through a farm gate to a metalled road. Turn left and go into **Newby**, with its attractive village green. Just after the end of the village, turn right along a narrow lane signed 'public bridleway'– **Laithbutts Lane** on the map. This is delightful walking. The lane briefly leads into fields but you can't go wrong if you keep in the same direction. Turn right when you come to a metalled road, and then left along **Eggshell Lane** into **Clapham**.

④ Just after an unsurfaced lane goes off on the left, turn left into a garden marked 'Ingleborough Cave'; this is the beginning of the route up to Ingleborough. It is a private path, and the entry cost was 40p at the time of writing. (If you object to paying this, you can go up the lane you have just passed, but you will miss an attractive stretch of the route.) The path goes past a

large lake and beside the deep valley of swift-flowing **Clapham Beck**. There is mature mixed woodland throughout, including some fine yews. The route then continues up the valley, passing Ingleborough Cave on the left and shortly afterwards a large hole in the ground which disgorges Clapham Beck. Continue up the wooded, now dry valley, which narrows dramatically in **Trow Gill** gorge. After a steep rocky climb, the path goes along a shallow valley, with a wall on the left.

⑤ After a ladder stile, you are in open country. (**Bar Pot** is passed on the left, and there is a fine view of **Ingleborough** ahead.) The limestone underfoot has now become peat. When the path divides, go right.

Behind the fencing ahead lies Gaping Gill. You will soon see the reason for the fencing: this is where Fell Beck disappears into an awesome gaping hole. A few hundred feet below, there is a cavern big enough to take York Minster – that is some size.

Rejoin the main path, and climb steeply up the side of **Little Ingleborough**.

Glance behind, and you will see Pendle Hill, while over to the right Penyghent dominates the scene, and beyond it is Buckden Pike.

After **Little Ingleborough**, the climb is mainly done, and the path soon reaches the top of **Ingleborough** at the right-hand side of the plateau.

Ingleborough is full of interest; it is pock-marked with pot holes, and on the top is an important Iron Age hill fort. Even on a cold day, it is worth lingering for a few minutes to appreciate the view from the top. Moving away from the summit shelter, stray close to the edges of the plateau, where in addition to the marvellous wide prospect of the Lake District fells and the Pennines, you will get good foreground views too. From the northern edge, there is a stunning view of Ribblehead viaduct. From further west round the edge, you can see Whernside and the extensive white stretch of clint and scars on its flank at Twistleton.

⑥ Be careful how you leave the summit when you are ready to descend, as the wrong path is easily taken. Go from the shelter to the trig point, and then veer slightly right to a big pile of rocks (a former hospice). The path is just to the left of this. For the first few yards, it is steep and rocky, but there are no problems after this, and a clear easy path goes down into the valley at **Crina Bottom**. (Straight ahead, the full expanse of **Morecambe Bay** delights the eye.)

⑦ **Crina Bottom** is a delightful place, and its green sward must be as good as any at Lord's or St Andrews. (Glance back for a marvellous view of Ingleborough, and Morecambe Bay is still in sight for most of the way.) After **Crina**, the path soon leads into a walled lane, which you follow into **Ingleton**.

Ingleton is a pleasant large village at the bottom of the valleys of the River Doe and the River Twiss. Both valleys have fine waterfalls. It comes as some surprise perhaps to discover that Ingleton was a coal mining village well into the 1930s.

Date walk completed: